You Are Witnesses of These Things

Sharing the Story of Jesus

Craig Alan Satterlee

Chelsey Satterlee

Arborvitae Books

Dewitt

You Are Witnesses of These Things
Sharing the Story of Jesus

Cover design: Chelsey Satterlee
Cover image: © korkeng via Canva.com

Library of Congress Control Number: 2022918552
Print ISBN: 979-8-9870603-0-8
EBook ISBN: 979-8-9870603-1-5

ARBORVITAE
BOOKS
DEWITT, MI

For our mothers

Helen M. Satterlee

Cathy Anne Schram Satterlee

Who shared with us the story of Jesus

Contents

Preface

As COVID-19 turns from pandemic to endemic, church leaders and churchgoers are returning to church and enticing other members to return with them. At the same time, church leaders and churchgoers are also returning to our preoccupation with the church's decline. How does the church return, first, to pre-pandemic attendance, giving, and participation, and then to evidence and a trajectory of growth? Depending on how we answer this question, the church may return to the defeat and despair about the future many church leaders and churchgoers felt prior to the pandemic.

Attempting to grow the church for the sake of the institution is such futile, tiresome work. Jesus said of the Jerusalem temple: "the days will come when not one stone will be left upon another; all will be thrown down."[1] Reflecting on Jesus's words, Craig once declared, "I do not want to spend my life propping up stones God has destined to fall." Trying to prevent the stones of the church as it is presently built from falling will certainly crush us.

Craig, a pastor, seminary professor, and bishop, was therefore delighted, even inspired when his church, the Evangelical

Lutheran Church in America (ELCA) recently identified its mission to "Share the story of Jesus and the ELCA by engaging with 1 million new people as we grow the church together."[2] Craig was excited to think of the ELCA sharing the story of Jesus with 1 million people who had not received it, and he embraced the story of the ELCA as a unique perspective on the story of Jesus that emphasizes grace and invites people, in this church's own words, to "know the way of Jesus and discover community, justice and love."[3]

Chelsey, a millennial raised with the story of Jesus but not personally engaged in the life of a congregation, sees a clear distinction between sharing the gospel and maintaining the institutional church. Chelsey was more skeptical about the ELCA's motivation for sharing the story of Jesus with 1 million new people and thought Craig was perhaps a bit naïve. Chelsey suspected the words "as we grow the church together" are the key to this mission, the goal is obtaining 1 million more members for the denomination, and sharing the story of Jesus is a strategy, a means to this end rather than the end itself. Craig has come to agree that Chelsey is correct.

Craig once believed that, if people become part of the church, they may become followers of Jesus. We are now convinced that the only reason new people will become part of the church is because they received the story of Jesus, want to learn more about or even become followers of Jesus and experience the church actively following Jesus. We are also convinced that, with all that is happening in society, the world, and their lives, people are open, even eager, to receive the story of Jesus and the good news that

God is working to bring unconditional love and abundant life to all creation. They are also watching and listening to determine whether the church is, indeed, following Jesus in this work in its own life and its witness in society.

As Chelsey's review and revision of Craig's drafts made this perspective prominent, this book became significantly stronger as writing evolved into a collaboration. So, while the author's voice in this book may be singular *I*, it is, in reality, the co-authors' plural *we*.

We wrote this book for Christians like Craig who are excited about telling the story of Jesus to people for whom it is new and have no interest in coercing or persuading people to become members of the church. More important, we wrote this book for people like Chelsey who are curious about God's presence and work in the world and have no interest in joining a church. We refer to the ELCA's mission statement for the ways it inspires Craig and are also honest about the skepticism Chelsey brings. Christians of other traditions might examine their own denomination's mission statement. For example, the Episcopal Church's statement on evangelism encapsulates much of this book: "Listen for Jesus' movement in our lives and in the world. Give thanks. Proclaim and celebrate it! Invite the Spirit to do the rest."[4]

We envision groups of Christians reading this book, discussing what they read guided by questions that conclude each chapter, practicing the skills taught in this book together, and providing each other prayer, feedback, and support. We urge groups to work through this book in a deliberate manner to give the Holy Spirit time and space to participate in the process. Taking time also helps us approach this work as a partnership with God bathed in prayer and not a course to be completed. To assist groups in this work, a reading guide is provided in the appendix. Learning to intentionally share the story of Jesus is a meaningful way for a congregation or synod to spend a year of its life.

We are confident that the approach we propose will be fruitful because Craig has used it with both high school students upon their return from mission trips and lay missionaries home on leave. By working through this process, these groups moved from sitting with blank pieces of paper to sharing their story of Jesus with one another in a two-hour seminar. We pray this book leaves those who read it and try it more hopeful, joyful, and confident in sharing their story of Jesus with others.

Chapter 1

"And They Worshiped Him"

You opened this book in response to a curiosity, an internal nudge, a quiet invitation, or an outright summons to witness to Jesus or to consider learning to witness to Jesus, in an intentional way. Thank you for taking this call prayerfully and seriously. People close to and around you, as well as our world, urgently need to receive the good news that Jesus loves them, brings them life, and is at work in the world to turn silence into speech, despair into hope, division into reconciliation, brokenness into wholeness, hatred into forgiveness and repentance, and death into life.

Luke 24 is filled with wonderful stories of Jesus fulfilling God's promises: the resurrection of Jesus by which God brings life out of death, the walk to Emmaus in which Jesus explains that God is present in and transforms suffering and hate, Jesus's appearance to the disciples, restoring them and giving them a second chance, and the ascension of Jesus by which Jesus leads the way to the time when the reign of God will be fulfilled. As Luke tells the story, in that single day, the disciples go from considering news of Jesus' resurrection an idle tale to understanding themselves as commissioned by the risen Lord as witnesses to these things.

Luke tells us how the disciples responded to their encounter with the risen Christ, Jesus's commission to be his witnesses, and the sight of Jesus carried up into heaven. "And they worshiped him."[1] The disciples worshiped Jesus. They were continually in the temple blessing God. They were devoting themselves to prayer.

Worshiping Jesus is how the Holy Spirit moves disciples from experiencing Jesus to witnessing to Jesus. This book is therefore best read prayerfully and among God's faithful people. This book is written presuming those who read it gladly partake of Jesus present in the word, remember the gift and call of baptism, sing God's praise, and, as appropriate, receive Jesus present in bread and wine. We will not tell or remind you to worship and pray. If these things were not part of your life, you would not be summoned, invited, or feel an internal nudge to witness to Jesus. By the grace of the Holy Spirit, as we worship, pray, and read this book, our hearts will burn within us, and, like Cleopas and his companion after their walk to Emmaus, we will get up joyously and excitedly to witness to Jesus. May our triune God grant us the faith and courage to find our voice.

Finding Our Voice

The Gospel of Luke reports that the people of Nain "glorified God, saying, 'A great prophet has risen among us!' and "God has looked favorably on his people!' This word about [Jesus] spread throughout Judea and all the surrounding country."[2] From angels telling shepherds who told the people of Bethlehem, to reports like this one of Jesus's public ministry, to women returning from the tomb and announcing Jesus is risen,[3] the good news of Jesus has been shared by word-of-mouth. Imagine if the good news ended the way Mark originally ended his gospel: "So [the women] went out and fled from the tomb, for terror and amazement had seized them; and they said nothing to anyone, for they were afraid."[4] Thankfully, those women spoke and, over the centuries, countless lives, including ours, were changed for the better. Because those women found their voice, the good news of Jesus was told and retold until someone told us.

"Preach the gospel at all times, and if necessary, use words." We often recall these words attributed to Francis of Assisi, which he never said, to excuse ourselves from talking about Jesus by suggesting that actions speak louder than words. We conclude that acts of love and service are the primary, even exclusive, way to share the good news. To the contrary, Francis fearlessly preached the gospel verbally to people he met. Besides, Paul makes clear that words are always necessary.

In Romans, Paul sums up the good news, "the same Lord is Lord of all and is generous to all who call on him. For, 'Everyone who calls on the name of the Lord shall be saved.'" Then, knowing Christianity is a word-of-mouth phenomenon, Paul asks, "But how are they to call on one in whom they have not believed? And how are they to believe in one of whom they have never heard? And how are they to hear without someone to proclaim him? And how are they to proclaim him unless they are sent? As it is written, 'How beautiful are the feet of those who bring good news!'"[5]

Today, perhaps for the first time in a long time, the world urgently needs the good news of God's pure and radical grace in Jesus Christ. "And I, when I am lifted up from the earth, will draw all people [some manuscripts say *creation*] to myself,"[6] Jesus declares. Jesus's words are a pronouncement of unconditional love and welcome for all people and all creation. Sharing this good news—telling people Jesus loves them, forgives them, values them, gives them a second chance when they need it, and intends for them to share in his own abundant life now and forever—is joyous and fun, especially when we expect nothing more than that they receive this good news.

To faithfully witness to Jesus, we must follow the example of the women in Mark's Easter story by overcoming our fear, finding our voice, and bearing witness to Jesus by speaking the good news. We must also embrace the truth that we do not convince or persuade anyone to believe in Jesus; we do not create, instill, or increase faith. Despite our best intentions, to attempt to convert someone might venture into coercion, manipulation, and making false claims and promises, all of which are contrary to the way of Jesus who gave people the freedom to turn away from him. Jesus said, "'For this reason I have told you that no one can come to me unless it is granted by the Father.' Because of this many of his disciples turned back and no longer went about with him."[7]

"No one can come to [Jesus] unless it is granted by the Father." Attempting to make someone have faith and respond to the gospel is inappropriate because this work belongs to God and not to us. Article VI of the *Augsburg Confession* (1530), the primary confession of faith of Lutheran Christians, declares: God "gives the Holy Spirit who produces faith, where and when [the Spirit] wills, in those who hear the gospel."[8] We are responsible to share the gospel, so people "hear" or receive the good news of Jesus. We hope and pray those who receive the gospel from us come to faith. We help them in every way, as the Holy Spirit gives us opportunity. To tell people of Jesus is to commit to and invest in them. To ask nothing in return is to extend the grace that Jesus shows us on the cross.

The Way of Jesus

The book of Acts uses the phrase "the Way" as the name by which the early Christian community identified itself.[9] To "know the way of Jesus" is to belong to the community of Jesus. Few people come to know Jesus apart from a Christian community. In fact, in the first centuries of the church, people came to know Jesus by first finding belonging in the Christian community, then learning to behave the way that community behaves, and only then believing what the community believes. Ideally, a Christian community's character and traits reveal who they believe Jesus is. For example, in the Evangelical Lutheran Church in America (ELCA), we declare that through knowing and following Jesus, people discover community, justice, and love.

As we tell the story of Jesus, we must be careful not to make the "Way of Jesus" a program or discipline we follow, or a doctrine or formula we accept, to find or receive Jesus. We do not present the "Way of Jesus" as the teachings of Jesus or the example of Jesus apart from the relationship with Jesus as Savior and Lord, which Jesus established in his life, death, and resurrection and assures us of in baptism. Jesus is "the way" of the truth that leads to abundant life.[10]

When asked about Jesus, we might naturally respond by talking about our church. This response is understandable since the church is the body of Christ in which many experience Jesus most deeply. Still, we must be careful that the story of any Christian community does not supplant the story of Jesus. We know that, when a Christian community does not reflect the way of Jesus, live up to expectations or reveals itself to be the gathering of human beings in need of Jesus, people's faith is challenged and undermined. This is even truer when the Christian community, rather than the Christ, has become the object of faith and devotion. Promoting the church as an institution is a related but a distinct conversation from sharing the good news of Jesus. The best way to preserve and promote the church is to reach out to people to whom the church is already important.

"You Are Witnesses of These Things"

"Then [Jesus] said to [the disciples], 'These are my words that I spoke to you while I was still with you—that everything written about me in the law of Moses, the prophets, and the psalms must be fulfilled.' Then he opened their minds to understand the scriptures, and he said to them, 'Thus it is written, that the Messiah is to suffer and to rise from the dead on the third day, and that repentance and forgiveness of sins is to be proclaimed in his name to all nations, beginning from Jerusalem. You are witnesses of these things. And see, I am sending upon you what my Father promised; so stay here in the city until you have been clothed with power from on high.'"[11]

We invite you to learn, even memorize, these verses from Luke's Gospel because they provide the inspiration for this experiment in sharing the story of Jesus. *You Are Witnesses of These Things* consists of four movements modeled after what the risen Christ said to the apostles immediately before the ascension: (1) Jesus opens our minds, (2) Jesus names us witnesses, (3) Jesus sends the promised Spirit, and (4) Jesus commands us to stay before we go.

Jesus "opened their minds to understand the scriptures." Jesus then used the Scriptures–the law of Moses, the prophets, and the psalms–to summarize his mission: "Thus it is written, that the Messiah is to suffer and to rise from the dead on the third day, and that repentance and forgiveness of sins is to be proclaimed in his name to all nations, beginning from Jerusalem." In the first part of our work, we learn about Jesus by opening our minds to the gospels, Apostles' Creed, and experience.

Jesus commissioned the apostles: "You are witnesses of these things." In the second part of our work, we learn how to talk about and bear witness to Jesus. We learn a method for preparing and writing our "testimony," and sharing it with one another. We consider the importance of sowing the seed of the gospel even when there is no harvest to gather. We undertake this work trusting it is a means through which Jesus sends the promised Holy Spirit upon us.

Jesus tells the apostles, "And see, I am sending upon you what my Father promised." The third part of this work is to pray over and practice our testimony in various ways, asking and trusting

Jesus is sending the promised Holy Spirit. This is also the time when the congregation readies itself to welcome those who may come to our church in response to our testimony. It is important that the Christian community to which we belong reflects what we say about Jesus.

Finally, Jesus said, "So stay here in the city until you have been clothed with power from on high." The apostles did not wait passively. "They were continually in the temple blessing God," they "were constantly devoting themselves to prayer," and getting themselves organized.[12] The fourth part of our work is to pray, plan, and build anticipation for our own Pentecost experience. Our plan includes identifying the person to whom we want to witness, praying specifically for that person, putting ourselves in an appropriate location for the conversation, witnessing to Jesus, and thanking Jesus for this gift of faith and discipleship. During this time, we also pray for ourselves and for one another, seek the congregation's prayers, and ask others to pray for and with us. At last, the Pentecost moment comes and we stand alongside the women returning from the tomb and Peter and the apostles as we share the story and way of Jesus with people who need to receive it.

Sharing the Story of Jesus Together

You Are Witnesses of These Things takes seriously that all the baptized bear responsibility for the proclamation of the gospel. We know the story of Jesus is fear-ending, death-defeating, life-giving, world-changing good news and together will explore how best to share it. We will experiment, embrace trial and error, succeed, and fail. And we will learn. As we do this work together, we must remember that the pastor plays an essential role, but is neither completely responsible for nor totally removed from the congregation witnessing to Jesus. The pastor is not Jesus and ought not be expected to be or regarded as Jesus. When this happens and the pastor inevitably disappoints or departs, the Christian community and the faith of its members may be put at risk.

To successfully share the story of Jesus with others, congregations and pastors must understand and support each other throughout the process of witnessing to Jesus. Pastors are often challenged to witness to people for whom the story and way of Jesus are new because the people they know best and interact with most belong to the congregation. Pastors must also remain vigilant for opportunities to bear witness to Jesus, whether to individuals or groups, and respond when those opportunities present themselves. To do this, pastors must be present in the community in ways that make them visible and available to people beyond the congregation. Since it takes time to establish and develop relationships beyond the congregation, time members often feel the pastor is taking away from them, congregational leaders should support their pastor's work of active engagement in the community as an important part of witnessing to Jesus.

Just as congregations support the pastor in sharing the story of Jesus, pastors also support the congregation by equipping them to witness to Jesus. Pastors fulfill this pastoral responsibility through preaching, teaching, modeling, praying, and supporting. Pastors preach about Jesus as the Savior who brings God's good news and, through the language they use in sermons, show and instruct the congregation how to talk about Jesus.[13] Pastors teach the Bible and a denomination's theology in ways that invite conversation, exploration, and engagement with people's lives and the world. Pastors also seek to strengthen and enliven faith by supporting witnessing to Jesus; pastors make the process and the individuals participating in it an important part of their ministry and the congregation's life. This support includes attending or leading gatherings of this process and praying for it personally and in the prayers of the congregation's worship. Ideally, the pastor does all these things regularly and so they are neither new nor extra work.

Pastors also support members of the congregation witnessing to Jesus by being available to become part of the conversation. When a congregation member witnesses to someone to whom the story and way of Jesus are new and a conversation begins, a time may come when the member feels unsure or unqualified to respond to the person coming to know Jesus. When this happens, the pastor is available to either coach the witness or enter directly into the conversation. Pastors make certain that those witnessing to Jesus know of their eagerness to partner in these ways.

Sharing the story of Jesus is more meaningful and joyous when we commit together not to be concerned about growing the church or pray the church will grow because of our sharing the story of Jesus, but instead entrust any growth to God. If our actual concern is prolonging the viability and life of our congregation, synod (diocese), or denomination, we do better to appeal directly to those for whom the survival of the institutional church is their ultimate concern. People new to the story of Jesus are interested in knowing Jesus as Savior, not in saving our church.

Since we are not growing the church, we can slow down. We can approach learning to share the story of Jesus as a journey of four legs. Ideally, this book will provide an action plan to follow. At the end of each leg, you can stop, pray, and decide whether to embark on the next leg of the journey. Do your best not to anticipate. Jesus says, "So do not worry about tomorrow, for tomorrow will bring worries of its own. Today's trouble is enough for today."[14] Today's decision is whether to open your mind to learn more about Jesus and increase your faith.

For Consideration and Conversation

1. Recall a time when someone told you about or reminded you of Jesus. Who was that person? What did they say?

2. What, if anything, makes you uncomfortable about talking about Jesus? What, if anything, excite you about talking about Jesus?

3. As you reflect on the itinerary outlined in this chapter, are there experiences you want to make certain you have along the way?

4. What prayer do you offer as you begin this process, what prayer do you need or desire?

5. Are you comfortable distinguishing between talking about Jesus and promoting the church? Why or why not?

Chapter 2

"He Opened Their Minds"

Jesus "opened their minds." Jesus illuminated the apostles. His intention was to enlighten them spiritually and not merely to give them knowledge and information. Similarly, as we consider Jesus's life, death, and resurrection, Jesus illuminates our minds, as well as our hearts and our lives, to his ongoing presence among us and in the world. Our purpose in contemplating Jesus is neither to pass a church test about Jesus nor to be able to answer people's challenging questions about Jesus. We intentionally provide Jesus the space in our hearts, minds, and schedules to make us keenly aware of his abundant life and empower us to witness to him.

In this chapter, we invite Jesus to use the gospels to illumine us to who Jesus is and what Jesus would have us tell others about him. In the two chapters that follow, we ask Jesus to use the Apostles' Creed and experience. We approach the gospels, creed, and experience, along with our knowledge and learnings of Jesus, ourselves, others, our community, and the world, as ingredients in the stew pot of our minds and hearts. Simmering over the fire of the Holy Spirit, these ingredients will produce a delicious testimony of what we have seen and heard of Jesus and what we believe about him. Witnessing to Jesus becomes serving this delicious stew to another.

The Gospels

Jesus opened the disciples' minds to understand Scripture – "the law of Moses, the prophets, and the psalms"– to comprehend that Scripture bears witness to Jesus.[1] While some question the propriety of "reading Jesus into the Hebrew scriptures," the gospels are unquestionably the testimonies of the witnesses we know as Matthew, Mark, Luke, and John. Luke makes this explicit, describing this gospel as "an orderly account of the events that have been fulfilled among us, just as they were handed on to us by those who from the beginning were eyewitnesses and servants of the word."[2] More precisely, the Gospel of Luke is a carefully investigated report of eyewitness testimonies.

The gospels teach us to witness to Jesus in four ways. First, the gospels demonstrate that our witness to Jesus is both similar and unique. Second, the gospels offer direction on how to witness to Jesus. Third, the gospels suggest people who would be receptive to receiving the story of Jesus. Fourth, the gospels provide stories of Jesus that are meaningful to us, stories that might inspire or form the basis of our witness.

Similar and Unique

The four gospels are similar in that they all narrate the life and ministry of Jesus, from the proclamation of John the Baptist to the resurrection. The synoptic gospels, Matthew, Mark, and Luke, describe events from a similar perspective, as contrasted with that of John. Despite this difference, these four gospels are similar enough that the Church includes them in the New Testament and regards them as faithful witnesses.

To fully appreciate the gospel witness, we benefit from re-familiarizing ourselves with their common story of Jesus. Reading the entire Gospel of Mark in a single sitting, preferably aloud with a group, is an effective way to experience the story of Jesus from start to finish before considering the gospels' uniqueness in smaller pieces and greater detail. While any of the gospels serve this purpose, Mark is the shortest and contains the most essential story of Jesus. A group might read Mark together by taking turns reading chapter by chapter.

The gospels are unique in that Matthew, Mark, Luke, and John tell the common story of Jesus to provide distinct witnesses to Jesus that are appropriate to their audience and circumstance. Matthew presents Jesus as Israel's long-awaited, promised Messiah, the King of all the earth. Matthew tells the story of Jesus by alluding to stories from the Old Testament, particularly Moses and the exodus, and referring to the Hebrew Scriptures. Matthew also desires to make the kingdom or reign of God accessible and comprehensible to all. For this reason, the expression "kingdom of heaven" appears 32 times in Matthew.

Mark presents Jesus as a suffering servant. Jesus refers to himself as the "Son of Man" or Son of Humanity. Others call Jesus the Son of God, but he keeps his identity as the Messiah secret and commands others to do the same. Mark stresses Jesus's message that the kingdom of God is breaking into human life now as good news. Jesus demonstrates the nearness of God's reign as teacher, exorcist, healer, and miracle-worker. Even more, Jesus is the Son whom God sent to rescue humanity by serving and giving his life for them. Mark's portrait is in keeping with Christian interpretation of Old Testament prophecy.

Luke portrays Jesus as the Son of God and Son of Humanity who seeks and saves the lost. By employing references to the stories of similar Greco-Roman divine savior figures, such as Roman emperors, Luke makes clear that Jesus is the greatest of all saviors. Jesus pursues those considered beyond God's love, cultivates forgiveness and compassion among his followers, and, in word and deed, teaches ethical wisdom that right-sides the world, restoring it to what God intends.

John presents Jesus as the Word of God, through whom all creation came into being, who becomes fully human to reveal God the Father to the world. Jesus talks openly about his divinity, echoing God's declaration to Moses, "I AM WHO I AM"[3] with seven "I Am" declarations of his own. John depicts Jesus as teacher, healer, prophet, and Messiah. Jesus's death on the cross is his glorification and return to the Father. Rather than predicting his Passion in terms of suffering, Jesus explains three times that on the cross he will be "lifted up" or exalted.

The four gospels highlight different events, details, and emphases to communicate what they believe about Jesus. Paging through the gospels while paying attention to the subheadings many Bibles provide is a simple way to appreciate each gospel's uniqueness. Notice subheadings that do not appear in every gospel. For example, only Matthew includes the visit of the magi and the escape to Egypt. Luke alone includes the parables of the Good Samaritan and the Prodigal Son. Like the gospel writers, we all have unique stories of Jesus that highlight what we believe about him.

We can also notice stories common to more than one gospel but incorporated at different places in each gospel. For example, the miraculous catch of fish is recorded early in Jesus's ministry by Luke and results in Peter, James, and John becoming disciples. John includes the miraculous catch of fish after the resurrection where it confirms that Jesus is indeed risen. Other gospel rearrangements are not this obvious. The invitation is to consider why a gospel writer places a story where it is and how the order of what we share about Jesus in our own witnessing can enhance what we believe about him.

The gospel writers' distinct portraits come to life when we compare the same story in each of the four gospels. We learn to shape our witnessing by including, omitting, or nuancing details. Jesus's baptism and death provide two examples. Mark's account of Jesus's baptism reports Jesus saw the heavens being torn open. The Spirit descended upon Jesus like a dove, and the voice from heaven spoke to Jesus. This was a personal, internal experience. Jesus's identity remains secret from everyone else in the story. In Matthew, John the Baptist attempts to prevent Jesus from being baptized by asserting that John needs Jesus to baptize him. Matthew tells us heaven was torn open, Jesus saw the Spirit of God descend and alight on him, and the voice spoke of Jesus for all to hear. Jesus is publicly proclaimed the long-awaited Messiah. Luke shows Jesus's concern for the lost by adding that Jesus was not baptized until everyone else had been baptized. The Holy Spirit descends upon him in bodily form as a dove. The voice speaks to Jesus for all to overhear. Jesus is not baptized in John's Gospel; John the Baptist simply points Jesus out as the Lamb of God who takes away the sins of the world.

Comparing the details of Jesus's death is also illustrative. In Mark, Jesus, the Suffering Servant, cried out in a loud voice, "My God, my God, why have you forsaken me?"[4] With a loud cry, Jesus breathed his last. Matthew reports that Jesus gave up his spirit. Matthew then describes signs of the coming of the Messiah: the curtain of the temple was torn in two, the earth shook and rocks split, tombs were opened, and holy ones who died came to life. A centurion proclaimed Jesus as the Son of God. In Luke, Jesus remained concerned for those considered lost; he assured one of those crucified with him that he will be with Jesus in paradise. Jesus called out with a loud voice, "Father, into your hands I commit my spirit."[5] When Jesus had said this, he breathed his last. Jesus's final words are in stark contrast to Mark. John reports Jesus, knowing God's will had been accomplished and Scripture had been fulfilled, said, "it is finished," bowed his head, and gave up his spirit.[6] Jesus was exalted.

By reviewing the similarities and differences in the gospels, we can understand the gospels as distinctive accounts written through each writer's own perspective and understanding of Jesus. The gospels are not objective news reports. They are neither accurate nor inaccurate, right nor wrong. The gospels are unique testimonies to Jesus, purposefully presenting what the gospel writers have seen and heard of Jesus and what they believe about him. The gospels invite us to share the story of Jesus in a unique way that testifies to what we have experienced and believe about Jesus.

How to Witness

We can read the gospels for examples and instructions for witnessing to Jesus, starting with Jesus's parables. Jesus uses the images and experiences of everyday life to bear witness to the reign of God. Jesus draws his parables from the most common things, including salt, light, yeast, a lamp, a jar, and a lost coin. Jesus employs images from nature: the birds of the air, the lilies and grass of the field, seeds, and a tree and its fruit. Jesus also uses human relationships including a master and a servant, a son and a father, and the host and guests at a banquet. Jesus describes the work of God's reign in terms familiar to his hearers: sowing and harvesting, daily labor, stewardship of a landowner's property. We learn from the parables that what we say about Jesus cannot be churchy but must reflect the world and experiences we share with those to whom we desire to witness.

Jesus tells us how to witness. In Matthew 10:5–16, Jesus instructs the twelve disciples when he sends them on their mission. In Luke 10:1-23, Jesus directs the seventy he sends ahead of him to proclaim the nearness of God's reign. Unlike the disciples and the seventy, we will probably not go to witness to Jesus carrying no money. However, we can eat and drink what those we visit provide and allow Jesus to send us "like lambs into the midst of wolves"[7] by cultivating a spirit of humility, vulnerability, and dependence upon Jesus and toward those to whom we witness.

Jesus does not separate spiritual and physical needs but is concerned for the whole person. In his public ministry, Jesus identified with members of society who were considered "the least" and made God known to them by healing, forgiving, sitting at the table with them, and teaching. Jesus revealed the power of service rather than dominance. Jesus's words are accompanied by actions that verify his teaching. Perhaps, for this reason, in Matthew, Jesus commissioned the disciples to respond to people's spiritual needs by making disciples, baptizing, and teaching and told them the final judgment will be measured by whether we responded to people's physical needs–feeding the hungry, clothing the naked, caring for the sick, and visiting the imprisoned.[8]

We do not choose between witnessing with words and witnessing with actions; the two are inseparable. We might hesitate to connect a simple act of kindness with the name of Jesus because that act does not compare to the mighty deeds of power Jesus performed. In response to our hesitation, Jesus says, "And whoever gives even a cup of cold water to one of these little ones in the name of a disciple—truly I tell you, none of these will lose their reward."[9] Moreover, a miracle is often best defined by the one who receives it rather than the one who performs it or those who observe it. People who are hungry sometimes experience the food they receive at a congregation's food pantry as miraculous. A simple gift of food might provide the occasion to bear witness to

Jesus using words. The size of the kindness does not matter. Making an explicit connection to Jesus does.

John demonstrates that witnessing requires time, patience, and repetition. At the end of his conversation with Jesus, Nicodemus is baffled. Jesus explained we enter the kingdom of God by being born anew or born from above. Nicodemus said to Jesus, "How can this be?" Jesus answered, "Are you a teacher of Israel, and yet you do not understand this?"[10] The conversation did not seem to go well. Yet, after the crucifixion, Nicodemus goes to Pilate with Joseph of Arimathea and requests Jesus's body. Together, they witness by burying Jesus lavishly as Messiah and king. Over time, Nicodemus moved from confusion to confession.[11]

John 20 shows the importance of repetition. The disciples need to receive the good news four times before they are ready to believe and witness that Jesus is risen. Early on the first day of the week, Mary Magdalene first brings the good news that she has seen the Lord. That evening, Jesus appears to the disciples in the house where they had met and shows them his hands and his side. A week later, Jesus again appears to them to include Thomas. Jesus comes to the disciples a fourth time by the Sea of Tiberias and gives them a miraculous catch of fish. At last, the disciples seem convinced that Jesus is risen and are ready to be his witnesses. Jesus is patient both with reticence to believe the gospel and reluctance to bear witness. This example shows that a single experience may not take hold and that rather than giving up, we graciously witness again. John 20 also illustrates that Jesus uses different approaches with the disciples. Jesus shows the disciples his hands and side. He invites Thomas to touch his hands inside.

By the Sea of Tiberius, Jesus provides the disciples miraculous catch a fish and, especially for Simon Peter, intimate conversation around a charcoal fire. Jesus shows us that we need to be ready to take a different tack as we witness to the same person.

While John's Jesus is patient for the disciples to respond to the good news, Mark's Jesus is urgent to share it. Mark reports an evening early in Jesus's ministry when the whole city was gathered around the door of the house where Jesus was staying; Jesus cured many who were sick and cast out many demons. In the morning, Jesus went to a deserted place by himself to pray. Simon Peter and his companions searched for Jesus, found him, and reported that everyone was searching for Jesus. Instead of returning with them, Jesus responded, "Let us go on to the neighboring towns, so that I may proclaim the message there also; for that is what I came out to do." Jesus went throughout Galilee, proclaiming the message in their synagogues and casting out demons.[12] Throughout Mark's Gospel, this urgency is punctuated by the repeated use of the word "immediately."

Jesus's urgency to share the good news is also evident in Matthew's and Luke's Gospels. In Matthew 10:14 and Luke 9:5, Jesus instructs those he sends out to shake from their feet the dust of towns that will not receive them. Unlike the example of patience and persistence we find in John, Matthew's and Luke's examples describe an urgency to share the gospel that compels us not to repeatedly try to persuade someone to receive and believe the story of Jesus, but instead to move on and continue to bear witness to others.

So how do we balance patience and persistence with eagerness and urgency? Finding the appropriate balance is always a matter of prayer since both patience and urgency can become justifications for ceasing to witness to Jesus. We might stop witnessing to others because we are patiently invested in a particular person. Or we might become so overwhelmed by the task that we find ourselves paralyzed. Prayer, especially prayer with others, will lead us to discern whether we are to continue to remain patient, move on, or seek creative ways to do both.

To Whom to Witness

We can read the gospels for clues to whom we might witness. We will not find specific people; however, individuals in the gospels indicate the kinds of people who would be receptive to the story of Jesus. The gospels certainly point us to people who know their need of God in tangible ways. Frequently, these people are sick, disabled, or, in the language of the gospels, "possessed by demons." Jesus cures, restores, and releases them. In a culture where sickness and disability are regarded as consequences of and even punishment for personal or familial sin, Jesus demonstrates God's compassion and love and bestows dignity. Jesus invites people who are physically sick, live with disabilities, and experience mental and emotional illness into his company, story, and way.

Jesus teaches us to do the same. Jesus says, "But when you give a banquet, invite the poor, the crippled, the lame, and the blind. And you will be blessed, because they cannot repay you, for you will be repaid at the resurrection of the righteous."[13] We cannot instantaneously and miraculously cure as Jesus did. In the name of Jesus, we can attest to God's love and compassion and that Jesus's will is for healing and wholeness. We can extend the dignity of being a child of God. We can invite these brothers and sisters to the banquet of the Lord and include them in our company and story as together we follow the way of Jesus.

John 3 and 4 introduces us to Nicodemus and the woman at the well who, each in their own way, long for God. We know people who, while not necessarily religious, are searching to experience and understand God. Jesus demonstrates the power of accompanying them on this quest as a conversation partner and listener. For both Nicodemus and the woman, dialogue itself is the experience of God. Understanding comes not as decision or realization but as illumination.

People who do not feel they belong are receptive to the story of Jesus. In Luke 19:1–10, Zacchaeus the chief tax collector longs to belong to the faith community. When Jesus said he must stay with Zacchaeus, Jesus empowered Zacchaeus to name who he truly is, not the crook people assumed but someone who gives half his possessions to the poor. When Jesus declared Zacchaeus a child of Abraham, Jesus restored him to the community. People who feel judged and excluded and desire more than membership in a congregation are more receptive to the story of Jesus. They want to be welcomed by a group of people among whom they can be their authentic selves and truly belong.

Hopefully, these examples are enough to inspire our thinking. We can read through the gospels looking first for named individuals and then kinds of people who gladly received Jesus's witness. Then we can ask ourselves and one another who these people are in our lives and communities. We might pray for them and think of them along with the gospel character who inspired our prayer.

Our Meaningful Gospel Story

The gospels may contain a story or stories that encapsulate our experience of Jesus and what we believe and want to share about him. This story or stories might inspire our own witness and be included in what we share. Some people can immediately identify and name their meaningful gospel story. Others must search for and discover it. Still others are delightfully surprised when they open themselves to this possibility and their story finds them.

We might quickly discover our meaningful gospel story by considering whether there is a character in the gospels that we especially appreciate and identify with. We might discover our meaningful gospel story by reading the gospels and paying attention to our hunches that a given gospel story might be our meaningful gospel story, and pausing to spend time with that story, reading it over and over. We consciously consider how the story speaks to and reflects our life, experience of Jesus, and belief about him. In this process, we will either settle on this story or realize we need to continue our search.

When we arrive at our meaningful gospel story, we record in writing why this story is meaningful and appropriate for us. We compose this reflection for ourselves. We control whether we share it, with whom, and how much we share. It is appropriate to prepare a simple answer to why this is our meaningful gospel story that we are comfortable sharing in case we are ever called upon to do so.

We also learn this story so that we can tell it accurately and meaningfully. We may even practice it aloud and, when we are ready, tell it to someone else. By telling a gospel story that is meaningful to us to someone, we are already witnessing to Jesus. Children are especially eager to hear stories that are important to us. Telling children our meaningful or favorite gospel story and why we love it is a powerful way to become comfortable witnessing to Jesus. Is this something we might try as a children's sermon?

For Consideration and Conversation

1. Using bullet points and working either individually or as a group create the story of Jesus without consulting a Bible or other resource. Work as quickly as you can. When you finish, review or your work. What do your inclusions and omissions tell you about what is important to you about Jesus?

2. Do you have a favorite gospel? What is it and why?

3. Pick someone in the gospels that Jesus interacts with. Imagine that you are their friend or neighbor and on hand when that person meets Jesus. What would you say to them afterward?

4. What gospel stories are especially meaningful to you? If you are comfortable, share the story and its meaning for you.

Chapter 3

The Church's Witness

Tradition or perhaps legend holds that, together, the apostles wrote a creed—a formal statement of belief—after Pentecost, before leaving Jerusalem to preach. The church has expressed its witness in creedal statements ever since this dubious beginning. Confessing with your lips that "Jesus is Lord"[1] is a creed. Many Christians continue to revere Philippians 2:6-11 as the ancient creed it is said to be:

> Christ Jesus, who, though he was in the form of God, did not regard equality with God as something to be exploited, but emptied himself, taking the form of a slave, being born in human likeness. And being found in human form, he humbled himself and became obedient to the point of death—even death on a cross. Therefore God also highly exalted him and gave him the name that is above every name, so that at the name of Jesus every knee should bend, in heaven and on earth and under the earth, and every

tongue should confess that Jesus Christ is Lord, to the
glory of God the Father.

Today, we begin our creedal statements with, "I believe..." or
"We believe..." and, with many other denominations, Lutheran
churches accept, teach, and confess the Apostles', Nicene, and
Athanasian Creeds. In the Lutheran tradition, we profess our faith
using the words of the Apostles' Creed at baptism and
confirmation and we confess the Apostles' or Nicene Creed most
Sundays in worship. The *Book of Concord* (1580), or the Lutheran
confessions, understands itself in relation to the creeds of the
ancient church. Each confessional document quotes or at least
mentions one of the ecumenical creeds [Apostles', Nicene, and
Athanasian].[2]

To learn to witness to Jesus, we can consider the creeds as the
Church's witness to who God is and what the Church believes
about God. Critiques of the creeds assure us that no witness or
testimony about God, Jesus, and the Holy Spirit is complete or
perfect. The creeds, then, are the Church's confession about the
triune God at a specific time in the Church's life, in response to
circumstances the Church faced.

The Apostles' Creed seems to represent some form of what the
early church called the "rule of faith," the core teachings of the
apostles that guided the early Christians. An early version of what
later became the Apostles' Creed, called the "Old Roman Creed,"
was in use as early as the second century. This is said to be the
creed the apostles composed together before leaving Jerusalem to
preach. The title "Apostles' Creed" is also mentioned about 390 by

Saint Ambrose, who refers to "the creed of the Apostles which the Church of Rome keeps and guards in its entirety."[3] What we now know as the Apostles' Creed is an enlargement of the Old Roman Creed, which first occurs, in a form nearly equivalent to its final form, in the early eighth century.

The Nicene Creed was the first creed to obtain universal authority in the church. In recognition and support of its official status, the *Augsburg Confession* declares that the decree of the Council of Nicaea (The Nicene Creed) is true and is to be believed without any doubt.[4] It improved the language of the Apostles' Creed by including more specific statements about the divinity of Christ and the Holy Spirit. The original Nicene Creed was adopted at the First Council of Nicaea in 325 to reject Arianism, which taught that Jesus, the Son of God, was the first-born of all creation, but only a creature—a godlike creature, but not God. The Nicene Creed regards Jesus as divine and co-eternal with God the Father. The Nicene Creed was amended at the First Council of Constantinople in 381 to include the Church's definitive statement about the divinity and co-equality of the Holy Spirit, the Third Person of the Trinity.

The Athanasian Creed originated in the late fifth century and, by the time of the Reformation, gained such prominence that it was considered equal to the Apostles' and Nicene Creeds as a confession of the true, catholic, and apostolic faith. The Athanasian Creed is a reaffirmation and clarification of the Nicene Creed. The first half of the Athanasian Creed is devoted to expressing the oneness of God according to God's "substance" and the threeness of God according to God's "persons." The latter half of this creed affirms that the second person of the Trinity is true God and true human united in the person of Jesus. The Athanasian Creed is rarely recited in worship, in part because it begins with statements about the necessity of believing it firmly and faithfully to be saved. We might benefit from approaching this creed as a poem that watches over us rather than a doctrine we must understand and accept.

In reflecting on the creeds, we also consider the *Augsburg Confession*. The third article of the *Augsburg Confession*, titled, "On the Son of God," expresses the reformers' belief about Jesus.[5] This article is in essence an echo and expansion of the second article of the Apostles' Creed. It teaches that the Word, the Son of God, assumed human nature in the womb of the blessed Virgin Mary, so two natures, the divine and the human, are inseparably conjoined in one person, one Christ—true God and true human being.

Article III quotes the creed in its exposition of the Son. Jesus was "born of the Virgin Mary," truly "suffered, was crucified, died, and was buried," so that Jesus might reconcile the Father to us, and be a sacrifice, not only for original guilt, but also for all human sin. Jesus also "descended into hell," and "on the third day" truly "rose again." Afterward Jesus "ascended into heaven to sit at the right hand of the Father," and forever reign and have dominion over all creatures. Jesus also sanctifies or makes holy all who believe in him, by sending the Holy Spirit into their hearts, to rule, comfort, and make them alive, and to defend them against the devil and the power of sin. The same Christ will publicly "come again to judge the living and the dead." Article III of the *Augsburg Confession* concludes, "according to the Apostles' Creed."

Today, a major concern with the creeds is their use of masculine language for God. An important theological rule is that God transcends both sex (biological differentiation) and gender (cultural meaning associated with sex). The creeds, which use the androcentric or masculine language of the Bible and Christian tradition, do not speak of God in humanly inclusive ways. God is ultimately mystery and beyond human speech. The claim of the creeds is that God became truly human and not that Jesus was a man.

Responding to the Creed

Preaching to those preparing for baptism at Easter, Saint Ambrose described the Old Roman Creed saying, "This Creed is the spiritual seal, our heart's meditation, and an ever-present guardian; it is, unquestionably, the treasure of our soul."[6] For Ambrose, the creed is the "treasure" the church has built up and draws upon to communicate the faith; the creed is a guardian because it protects us from error. Adding to Ambrose's reflection, the creed is precious because reciting it is a remembrance of our baptism and a way we commune with the saints. Praying the creed is a protection from those things that would take us away from God. As the meditation of our heart, reflecting on the creed can stimulate, shape, and empower our witness to Jesus.

The Second Article of the Apostles' Creed tells us succinctly who Jesus is – God's only son, our Lord, conceived by the Holy

Spirit and born of the Virgin Mary – and what Jesus did. Meditating on the Second Article and journaling our reflection might inspire what we say when we witness to Jesus. In one sense, this is what Martin Luther did.

Though we primarily think of Luther's catechisms as instructions, the catechisms are also Martin Luther's reflections on his experience of God as informed by the essential teachings of the Christian faith. Both catechisms provide reflections on the Apostles' Creed, including contemplations on who Luther experiences Jesus to be and what Luther believes about Jesus.

Many people who grew up as Lutheran Christians learned their understanding of the Apostles' Creed from Luther's *Small Catechism* (1529) in confirmation class. We can look to Luther's explanation of the second article as an example and even a model of how to witness to Jesus.[7] Luther begins by reinforcing what the Church through the creeds intended to address; "that Jesus Christ [is] true God, begotten of the Father in eternity, and also a true human being, born of the Virgin Mary." Jesus is truly divine and truly human.

Luther then becomes very personal, bearing witness to who Jesus is to him and to us. Luther calls Jesus "my Lord," and explains that Jesus "has redeemed me, a lost and condemned human being. He has purchased and freed me from all sins, from death, and from the power of the devil, not with gold or silver, but with his holy, precious blood and with His innocent suffering and death."[8] Finally, in very personal terms, Luther describes why Jesus did this for him and for us: "He has done all this in order that I may belong to him, live under Him in his kingdom, and serve him in eternal righteousness, innocence, and blessedness, just as he is risen from the dead and lives and rules eternally."[9]

In the *Large Catechism* (1529), Martin Luther witnesses that, in Jesus, God has completely given Godself to us, withholding nothing. Luther encapsulates his testimony of Jesus in the words, "in Jesus Christ our Lord."[10] Luther provides a simple and straightforward testimony, which he instructs us to use: "I believe that Jesus Christ, true Son of God, is my Lord." Jesus is Lord because, in unfathomable goodness and mercy, Jesus came from heaven to help us. Jesus is Lord because Jesus routed and replaced the tyrants of evil, disobedience, and death and becomes the Lord of life, righteousness, and every good and blessing. Jesus is Lord because Jesus frees us from sin, death, and the devil, restores us to God's favor and grace, claims us as his own, protects and shelters us, and governs us by his righteousness, wisdom, power, life, and blessedness.

For Luther, "Lord" is shorthand for the One who has brought us back from evil to God, from death to life, from sin to righteousness, and keeps us safe. Luther explains that the remainder of the Second Article expresses how Jesus did this and at what great cost: becoming human, suffering, dying, and rising, swallowing up death forever by rising from the dead, and ascending to rule at the right hand of God.

Some meditate on the second article of the creed and are drawn to what is missing: the public ministry of Jesus. They prefer the creed read, "…born of the Virgin Mary, healed the sick and suffering, preached good news to the poor, shared table with outcasts and sinners, suffered under Pontius Pilate…." While acknowledging Jesus's works may be helpful in our understanding of Jesus, the omission of Jesus's public ministry makes clear that Jesus is God-with-us who saves by dying, rising, and ascending.

Yet, some feel we should not consider the cross apart from Jesus's public ministry, since Jesus's entire life is salvific. Jesus saves by identifying with members of society considered "the least" and revealing the God of love and life to them through healing, forgiveness, table fellowship, and embodying an understanding of power based on service rather than domination. Jesus gathered those considered beyond God's love and concern into community with himself and, therefore, with God.

"I believe in Jesus Christ, God's only Son, our Lord, who was conceived by the Holy Spirit, born of the virgin Mary, suffered under Pontius Pilate, was crucified, died, and was buried; he descended to the dead [or, "he descended into hell," *another translation of this text in widespread use*]. On the third day he rose again; he ascended into heaven, he is seated at the right hand of the Father, and he will come to judge the living and the dead."[11]

What is your reflection? The Second Article of the Apostles' Creed can help us better witness to Jesus. Read it repeatedly. Recite it throughout the day. Meditate on it as you pray to Jesus. Reflect on what it means for you. Realize that, when you say the creed in worship, you are already witnessing to Jesus.

For Consideration and Conversation

1. What, if anything, in the Second Article of the Apostles' Creed do you believe with conviction? What, if anything, in

the Second Article of the Apostles' Creed do you question? What, if anything, in the Second Article of the Apostles' Creed do you need the Church to believe for you?

2. If you were teaching confirmation, what one thing would you want your students to keep and remember about the Second Article of the Apostles' Creed?

3. How might the church revise or improve the Second Article of the Apostles' Creed so that it better speaks to the world today?

Chapter 4

The Witness of Experience

Women at a tomb are terrified by two men in dazzling white. Two disciples recognize Jesus in a stranger who blesses and breaks bread at their table. Disciples are startled by dead Jesus, alive and in the flesh, with pierced hands and feet. Our encounters with Jesus may not be as miraculous or spectacular as those of the disciples in Luke 24, but we have experiences of Jesus, nonetheless.

We usually cannot name an encounter with Jesus in the moment. We need to recall the experience and reflect upon it to become aware and convinced that we encountered Jesus. In the tomb, the two in dazzling clothes tell the women to remember what Jesus told them while he was still in Galilee; the women remembered Jesus's words, returned from the tomb, and witnessed to the eleven and to all the rest. Recognizing Jesus in the breaking of the bread, Cleopas and his companion recalled how their hearts burned within them when Jesus opened the scriptures to them on the road to Emmaus.[1] When our minds are opened to understand the scriptures, and our hearts are illumined by meditating on the creed, we are more attuned to these experiences.

Relating our experience of Jesus to others is especially powerful because it leads to others receiving an encounter with Jesus rather than information about Jesus.

Encounters with Jesus frequently affect us emotionally. Luke 24 uses emotion-laden verbs to describe disciples' reaction to Jesus. The women at the tomb are perplexed and terrified. The disciples are startled, terrified, joyous, disbelieving, and still wondering. After the ascension, they are filled with great joy and continually blessing God. Experiences that leave us feeling amazed, grateful, loved, sorry, forgiven, welcomed, afraid, or empowered might be encounters with Jesus, especially when we recall those experiences, continue to feel the emotions, and Jesus comes to mind.

Luke 24 points to places where Jesus encounters us: the tomb, the gathering of disciples where Jesus showed his hands and feet, the events of the day as discussed by travelers on the road; and the home and table of two disciples. These instances inspire us to consider our experience of Jesus in corresponding locations: places where we expect to find death but are surprised by new life, the church, our home and neighborhood, and the events of the world. Of course, these are but a starting point and not an exclusive list. Luke 24 demonstrates that Jesus encounters us wherever we need him.

Tomb

The tomb is perhaps the place we need Jesus most. Anyone who has left a loved one's casket at the grave or placed their cremains in the columbarium knows we leave a part of our own heart there as well. We have lost our loved one and we have lost who we are in relation to our loved one. Staring into the tomb we see only death. We question whether the heavy veil of grief will ever lift. We wonder what our life will be like from now on and whether we will ever again be joyous, happy, and hopeful.

Physical death is not the only tomb we experience. We can find ourselves locked away in the tomb of divorce or the end of a significant relationship. We can find ourselves shrouded in the grief caused by the loss of a physical ability, the separation or rejection of a community, and the termination of a career or the end of a vocation that provided us with identity and meaning. We can become disheartened, despairing, or indifferent because of the societal and systemic tombs that bury so many lives.

Just when it seems evil will reign victorious and death will have the last word, we experience a glimmer of hope, a promise we can hold onto, a sign of new life that we did not conjure or expect. Christians name this the presence and power of Jesus conquering death, rolling away the stone, allowing the light of God's grace to shine within the tomb, and exercising the power of his resurrection to transform death to new life. Paul writes, "Finally, beloved, whatever is true, whatever is honorable, whatever is just, whatever is pure, whatever is pleasing, whatever is commendable, if there is any excellence and if there is anything worthy of praise, think about these things."[2] As we think on these things, we are likely to recall the times when Jesus encountered us at the tomb.

Church

Perhaps the most obvious place to examine for experiences of Jesus is the church. The story of Jesus and the story of the church are not two but one related story. Sometimes, the story of the church leads into the story of Jesus; people experience the church's community and ministry in tangible ways and this experience provides the entrée for sharing the story of Jesus. Sometimes the story of the church results from the story of Jesus; people receive the story of Jesus and are curious; they seek out the church to experience the community, justice, and love Jesus brings. Either way, the story of the church is always in service to the story of Jesus; the story of Jesus is never in service to the story of the church.

The church is more than the congregation. The Evangelical Lutheran Church in America (ELCA), for example, intentionally expresses its faith, life, witness, and service in three ways: congregation, synod (diocese or district), and national and global ministries stewarded by a churchwide organization based in Chicago. These three "expressions" are interdependent and not hierarchical. Ideally, they function according to which expression is best able to carry out a particular aspect of the church's mission. Weekly worship, for example, is best accomplished in the congregation. Most people therefore feel the strongest bond to their congregation; however, people may feel primarily connected to the church through the synod and churchwide organization during certain seasons of their lives. A high school student, for example, might feel more connected to the denomination because of their experience at a national youth gathering than to their congregation at home.

When reflecting on our experience of Jesus in the church and telling the church's story, we consider all three expressions–congregation, synod, and churchwide ministries. To do this, we may need to learn about and experience our synod and the denomination. In addition to our own research, we might invite the bishop or a member of the synod staff to join us in conversation. We can also watch the videos our denomination produces.

Worship is the first place to reflect on how you experience Jesus in the church. How does Christ encounter you in word, sacrament, liturgy, and music? The ELCA mission says that, by knowing the way of Jesus (or the Christian community), people will discover community, justice, and love. Other denominations and even others within the ELCA highlight forgiveness, reconciliation, service, and vocation. So, worship, community, justice, love, forgiveness, reconciliation, service, and vocation provide categories for identifying our experience of Jesus in the church. We consider each of the church's three expressions because, as weekly worship finds its home in the congregation, other categories of experience are more obvious or prevalent in the synod or denomination.

Home and Family

Where, if anywhere, do we experience Jesus in our home? Jesus reveals himself to some people at the family table, as he did after walking with two disciples from Jerusalem to Emmaus. Others experience Jesus in the bath or shower where they remember the gift of baptism. Some experience Jesus in the place where they read the Bible and do their devotions each day. We might experience Jesus in a picture, cross, or crucifix hanging on the wall. For some, Jesus is outside in the garden, where they care for God's creation and remember the Word through whom all things came into being. For others, Jesus is in the craft room or the kitchen as they join Jesus in the work of creating. Other than church, if the place you experience Jesus is not in your home, where, if anywhere, is it?

Families are larger than those biologically related to us. Our *family* might be the people closest to us whom we care about the most; our family might be those with whom we share our time, our work, and our life. Jesus defines *family* as "those who hear the word of God and do it."[3] Sometimes, we experience Jesus in a member of our family, either by loving and caring for them or in the love and care that family member gives us. Reflecting on how Jesus is with us in those closest to us often results in gratitude for people we might take for granted.

The words Luther uses in the catechisms to describe Jesus's actions can stimulate our awareness of Jesus at work in those closest to us. In Chapter 3, we read from the *Large Catechism* that, in Jesus, God completely gives Godself to us, withholding nothing. Jesus reveals God's unfathomable goodness and mercy. Who are the family members that completely give themselves to us and withhold nothing from us? When have we experienced incomprehensible love for or from a member of our family? Luther also says Jesus helps us, restores us to favor and grace (or forgives us), takes us as his own, protects and shelters us. How do these gifts from members of our family reveal and inform our experience of Jesus?

Neighborhood

To experience Jesus in the neighborhood we either step out of our church, home, and family into the neighborhood and community, or we welcome the neighborhood and community into our church, home, and family. Whichever we choose, or if we undertake to do a bit of both, our purpose is to encounter Jesus in the neighborhood and not to presume to bring Jesus to the neighborhood. Consequently, we welcome the neighborhood into our home or church to listen to our neighbors, to hear their stories, and to receive their questions, objections, beliefs, and needs, not to make disciples and teach. To make disciples and teach, we welcome regular worshipers more deeply into our homes and churches.

Though somewhat unnerving, stepping out of the places where we are comfortable and venturing into the neighborhood is more adventurous and fun. We allow ourselves the joy of discovering Jesus in the neighborhood for ourselves rather than receiving reports from our neighbors as we sit in our churches. After we spend time in the neighborhood, we are in a better position to invite our neighbors into our church or home, and they are more likely to accept our invitation.

We engage the neighborhood trusting Jesus's words as he went, words Jesus instructed those he sent to proclaim. Matthew describes the beginning of Jesus's ministry: "From that time Jesus began to proclaim, 'Repent, for the kingdom of heaven has come near.'"[4] Later in his ministry, Jesus sends the disciples out with instructions to "proclaim the good news, 'The kingdom of heaven has come near.'"[5] In the neighborhood, we actively investigate where the reign of God has come near–what God is doing, and the new reality Jesus brings. Our aim is to discover, name, and describe it; our purpose is not yet to announce it, and certainly not to call for repentance. As in the gospels, expressions of awe, amazement, and praise might be our natural response to what Jesus is doing.

Jesus's public ministry provides clues to where we might encounter Jesus in the neighborhood. We can visit places of teaching, healing, welcome, and places where people tell us miracles occur. Jesus declares his presence in the hungry, thirsty, naked, sick, prisoner, and stranger. We can approach these neighbors as if they are Jesus himself; we can engage them as teachers and guides who can point us to the inbreaking of God's reign in the neighborhood. This is equally true for neighbors who are children, students, refugees, live with disabilities, are ethnically diverse, and have been told they are undeserving of God's love. Neighbors who are vulnerable and know their need of God are the most qualified to teach us where the reign of God comes near in our neighborhood.

Of course, to experience Jesus in the neighborhood, we need to change our self-understanding from those who possess the gospel and have something to give people in need of Jesus to people who are eager to receive because we know our need of Jesus. We make this shift by acknowledging that our experience of Jesus is always limited and incomplete. When we intentionally change our perspective, places in our neighborhood where we thought we serve—schools, food pantries, community meals, homeless shelters, college campuses, senior living centers, and so many others—become locations where we encounter Jesus.

We also need to be ready for Jesus to encounter us in the neighborhood anywhere, anytime, and not allow ourselves to be caught unprepared. Jesus says, "But know this: if the owner of the house had known at what hour the thief was coming, he would not have let his house be broken into."[6] When we step back from the story and reflect upon it, the Messiah comes in the most unexpected place of all: "wrapped in swaddling clothes, and lying in a manger."[7] We need to be ready for Jesus to encounter us where we least expect him: at the grocery store, on the bus, in the park, at a concert, or at a club.

World

"For God so loved the world that he gave his only Son, so that everyone who believes in him may not perish but may have eternal life. Indeed, God did not send the Son into the world to condemn the world, but in order that the world might be saved through him."[8] The word *world* or in Greek *cosmos* is used ten times in the Gospel of John to mean several different things. *World* or *cosmos* can mean the planet or physical earth, the entire universe, and the people of the world.[9] *World* can mean the world system (political and social structures), as when Jesus says, "Now is the judgment of this world; now will the ruler of this world be cast out."[10] John sometimes means the lost and alienated world, separated from God, that Jesus came not to condemn but to save. Jesus judges the world and casts out the world's ruler by being lifted up on the cross and suffering with the world.

John's multi-faceted use of the word *world* expands our experience of Jesus beyond church, home, family, and neighborhood. We can open ourselves to the Word through whom all things came into being by considering those things, especially the natural world, as revealing Jesus. Jesus is with and in all the peoples of the world, especially those who need to be saved from this world and those who this world condemns. We might experience Jesus by focusing on a country or region of the world to which we are connected or in which we are interested. Jesus judges all the systems and structures of the world that are alienated and separated from God. We might invest ourselves in an issue facing the world that we care about. The cross proclaims that Jesus is present in every place of suffering; Jesus is experienced in every glimpse of new life. We might look into rather than away from suffering in this world.

Our ways of experiencing Jesus in the world are as boundless as ways of experiencing the world. To encounter Jesus in church or religion apart from the world is an incomplete experience of Jesus. Our hope, therefore, is to encounter Jesus far from the church or at least not confined to the church. For, when we can tell the story of Jesus in ways that connect with the world, people may discover that, wherever we are, "In him we live and move and have our being'."[11]

For Consideration and Conversation

1. Has Jesus ever encountered you in a tomb in your life? How did you know he was there?

2. Can you think of an instance when the church's ministry led to sharing the story of Jesus? Can you think of an instance when sharing the story of Jesus resulted in someone seeking out the church?

3. Where have you experienced Jesus most in your congregation? Have you encountered Jesus in your synod or diocese and our national church? How?

4. Where do you encounter Jesus in your home?

5. Can you think of a time you experienced Jesus' love in the love of a member of your family?

6. Where in your neighborhood or community is the first place you would look for Jesus? Why?

7. If you could send Jesus anywhere in the world, where would you send him? Why?

Chapter 5

"You Are Witnesses"

"You are witnesses," Jesus tells the disciples.[1] We usually think of witnesses interviewed on the news or taking the stand in court. They have seen or heard something, and a reporter shoves a microphone in their face, or a lawyer issues them a subpoena, and they really do not have a choice whether to share. Jesus does something similar to the disciples. Jesus does not ask the disciples if they want, feel called, or possess the skills to witness. Jesus names the disciples witnesses, promises to send them power, and tells them to spend time together before setting out.

As Christians, and as a church, we are bound to honestly consider whether we who have experienced Jesus, received his grace, and share in his own abundant life can legitimately choose whether or not to witness to these things. Lutheran Christians spend so much time attempting to convince ourselves to witness to Jesus that we never quite get around to actually witnessing. Like Jesus's first disciples, we really do not have a choice. We have seen and heard these things of Jesus. While no one has issued a subpoena, in baptism Jesus nudges, invites, and summons us to share. Witnessing to Jesus may be something we are uncomfortable doing or afraid to do; witnessing to Jesus is not something we can choose not to do. Jesus bids us to take time and learn what it is to be a witness, the things we are witnesses of, and how to prepare our testimony, even as Jesus promises to send upon us power from on high.

What is a Witness?

"You are witnesses of these things." How do you suppose the disciples responded to Jesus's words? Perhaps they were relieved that Jesus quickly ascended away. What is your reaction to thinking of yourself as a witness to Jesus? We are frequently reluctant, even afraid, to witness to Jesus because the one with whom we share the story of Jesus might ask us a question we cannot answer, not join the church, or distance themselves from us because we make them uncomfortable. Our apprehension to speak about Jesus would be understandable, even appropriate, if Jesus had named us teachers, experts, recruiters, or anything else for which we must prove our qualifications and produce results. However, Jesus does not name us any of these things. Jesus calls us witnesses.

From prison, John the Baptist sent two disciples to ask Jesus, "Are you the one who is to come, or are we to wait for another?" Jesus answered, "Go and tell John what you have seen and heard." Jesus made John the Baptist's disciples his witnesses. As Jesus said to John's disciples, so Jesus says to us: "Go and tell what you have seen and heard."[2] This is what it means to witness. As Jesus's witnesses, we testify to what we have seen, heard, and experienced of Jesus, and we confess what we believe about it.

We might protest that we do not know enough to witness to Jesus. However, having all the answers is not important. As witnesses, we share about a person and relate an experience; we do not explain a doctrine or argue a case. People witness to restaurants all the time without being chefs, to movies without being cinematographers. They describe their experience, what they believe or how they feel about it, and why. We do this same thing as witnesses to Jesus. The most important thing when sharing the story of Jesus is that we believe what we are saying and say what we believe. Acknowledging when we do not know something may, in fact, strengthen our witness.

We might protest that we tried to talk to people about Jesus and none of them joined the church. As much as our church wants or needs more members, our purpose when witnessing to Jesus is not to "grow the church." We plant the seed of the gospel so the Holy Spirit can, perhaps in time, bring growth. We may never see this growth or benefit from it in our expression of the church.

Accepting that we are not likely to harvest what we plant helps us be witnesses to Jesus and not salespeople for the church. While we might share about the church as the way of Jesus or speak about it as a gathering of disciples in which Jesus's presence, power, and activity are manifest in community, justice, and love, we do not promote the church as a product, commodity, service, or worthwhile investment. Our goal in witnessing is not that people join the church, or even believe what we say, but that they receive the story of Jesus.

We might protest that we do not want to be one of *those* witnesses. We have been unnerved, angered, and offended by Christians who want to talk about salvation, the fires of hell, our mortal souls, and deciding in the moment to accept Jesus Christ as one's personal Lord and Savior. "If you were to die tonight, do you know where you are going?" We do not want to do that to our family and friends. We do not want to risk losing relationships that are important to us by making people dear to us uncomfortable. Thankfully, we are not talking about the fires of hell, mortal souls, and deciding for Christ. We are sharing the story of Jesus.

If people are going to distance themselves from us because we share the story of Jesus with them, they probably are not appropriate people for us to witness to, at least not yet. We witness to people who know us, appreciate us, perhaps admire us. We witness to people we know, care about, and with whom we want to share something precious. During his public ministry, perhaps Jesus told the seventy he sent ahead of him to stay in people's homes and eat at their tables, in part so the people would get to know the disciples and the disciples would get to know the people.[3]

An established relationship with someone or belonging to the same circle—neighborhood, school, work, recreation—often makes us a more trustworthy and effective witness. We are certainly more trustworthy than Christians who introduce themselves to people and immediately begin speaking of Jesus in an aggressive, manipulative, or judgmental manner. Witnesses with ulterior motives, including getting people to join their church, may be subtler but can be equally off-putting. Many therefore find the friend or neighbor who shares the story of Jesus with them with no hidden agenda much more effective than pastors, whom they regard as paid or professional witnesses like expert witnesses in a trial.

When we witness to people we care about, we do so in a way that honors them and preserves our relationship. We are likely to know something of their life and circumstances and be able to share the story of Jesus in a way that connects with them. We are also more likely to communicate that our motives are honorable; we desire nothing more than they know Jesus loves them, wants the best for them, joins them in everything they face, and includes them in his own abundant life, because they are precious to God, and nothing can change that. The challenge is to resist both expecting a response and giving advice about how to make life better or how to fix problems revealed by the one to whom we are speaking. Advice is best saved for another conversation, so we might offer to pray instead.

Whether interviewed on the news, testifying in court, posting a review on a blog, or telling the story of Jesus, all witnesses narrate events and provide a confession of belief; we tell what we have seen and heard and confess what we believe about it. At their best, witnesses communicate the specific, concrete event they witnessed without attempting to coerce or manipulate. By their testimony, witnesses invite others to enter their world and see it as they see it.

Witnessing to Jesus rests on faith rather than proof. Witnesses communicate conviction rather than certainty; we share what we believe and do not declare the way things are. Witnesses to Jesus know it is impossible to prove whether what we say is true or false;

people can only believe or reject it. Some witnesses find it helpful to include the phrase "for me" as they share what they believe about the story of Jesus.

Witnessing to Jesus is a wonderful practice because it is open to all believers. We do not need to be licensed, authorized, or ordained to tell the story of Jesus to the people around us. All Christians can deepen their own faith and the faith of others by witnessing to Jesus through the way we live and express our faith, and by directly sharing the story of Jesus with others.

"These Things"

"Thus it is written, that the Messiah is to suffer and to rise from the dead on the third day, and that repentance and forgiveness of sins is to be proclaimed in his name to all nations, beginning from Jerusalem. You are witnesses of these things."[4] Of all the things the disciples could tell people about him—his teaching, healing, miracles, and table fellowship, Jesus directs the disciples to bear witness to *these things*–Jesus's crucifixion and resurrection, and what God has done for us because of them.

How do we talk about Jesus's suffering, death, and resurrection? The church's pat answer is to say Jesus died on the cross to save us from our sins. This is indeed true. But what does this mean to people who do not know the story of Jesus, may not regard themselves as sinners, and are not concerned about spending eternity in hell? If we must convince people of the worldview assumed by this answer and condemn them as sinners in order that they might be saved, we miss the opportunity to share

Jesus's suffering, death, and resurrection in ways that address the helplessness, fear, worry, shame, futility, and, yes, death people struggle with as part of everyday life. So, how do we talk about Jesus's suffering, death, and resurrection?

The gospel writers provide different understandings of Jesus's death and resurrection; we find even more if we examine the epistles. We can embrace those that resonate with us as relevant to life in the world today. To begin, we can reflect on passages in which Jesus, or the gospel writers speaking through Jesus, express the meaning and significance of Jesus's suffering, death, and resurrection.

Repentance and Forgiveness: In Luke 24, Jesus tells the disciples to bear witness to his suffering, death, and resurrection by proclaiming "repentance and forgiveness of sins in his name." We are to tell the story of Jesus, which leads to a change of mind or heart (repentance) and the good news that in Jesus we find forgiveness. Jesus is clear that "repentance and forgiveness of sins is to be proclaimed in his name *to all nations, beginning from Jerusalem.*"[5] The good news of Jesus is universal in its scope and particular in its articulation. God's action in Jesus's suffering, death, and resurrection is good news for all people, for all creation, without exception.

A Ransom for Many: Jesus says, "For the Son of [Humanity] came not to be served but to serve, and to give his life a ransom for many."[6] Jesus's mention of a "ransom" indicates that his death does something; Jesus's death secures a release, but not in the way we typically think of when we hear the word *ransom*. While the Old Testament sometimes uses "ransom" to refer to a redemption or purchased freedom, "ransom" just as often refers to God's action to deliver people.[7] Jesus does not make a payment. Jesus's death does not repay either the penalties accrued by human sin, or something owed to God. Jesus's death delivers people.

We know Jesus's death delivers rather than pays off because Jesus talks about his death as a ransom while discussing power and subservience, not sin and the need to secure forgiveness. In this instance, "ransom" is a liberation produced by divine strength, not by payment. Without explaining how, Jesus declares that God, through Jesus's death, will free people from oppression and captivity to other powers, including both the social and political power that human beings construct to control each other and demonic powers that enslave the world and resist God's purposes. Jesus defeats the power of death itself and raises people to the community that reveals God's reign in this world through the power of servanthood.

Jesus's use of the word "many" is not meant to exclude but to emphasize the contrast between service in this world and service in God's reign. In this world, many serve one. In the reign of God, the One serves many by acting on their behalf. Jesus's use of the word "many" has the sense of "all" or "everyone," which is in keeping with the cosmic scope of Mark's Gospel.

New Life from Death: In John's Gospel, Jesus says, "'Now is the judgment of this world; now the ruler of this world will be driven out. And I, when I am lifted up from the earth, will draw all people to myself.' He said this to indicate the kind of death he was to die."[8] These verses are part of what Jesus declares to the world about his death, resurrection, and ascension.[9] This message is not just for

Jesus's disciples and the church. Looking closely at the verses, we understand Jesus is speaking about how his death will bring new life to the world. In stating, "Now is the judgment of this world," Jesus shares that, as his death is drawing near, this is the world's last opportunity to hear Jesus's words and believe in him.

Jesus further explains that now is also the time when "the ruler of this world will be driven out," which opens the way for new life with God. In John's Gospel, "the ruler of this world" is shorthand for Satan, evil within us, and powers and systems opposed to God. "After Satan entered into [Judas]," the ruler of this world is cast out of Jesus's presence when, "after receiving the piece of bread, [Judas] immediately went out. And it was night."[10] The ruler of this world was driven out of the light and into the darkness. Although in the Garden Jesus is handed over to the ruler of this world at work in the powers and systems opposed to God, the ruler of this world is ultimately driven out when Jesus is not condemned but exalted and glorified on the cross and raised from death to new life. Neither the evil within nor the evil around us wins. Jesus transforms them to new life.

Turning to the final verse, the phrase "the kind of death he was to die" elicits crucifixion but also suggests "the kind of death" that leads to Jesus's resurrection and ascension. When Jesus is "lifted up from the earth" to draw all people to himself, this lifting up is simultaneously crucifixion or lifting up on the cross, resurrection or lifting up from death, and ascension or lifting up to the Father. Jesus announces to the world, which knows death all-too-well, that in him death leads to resurrection or new life and ascension or life with God. To trust Jesus's words is to live in a way that leads not to death as the end but as the way to new life with God.

Express God's Love: Jesus says to the disciples, "No one has greater love than this, to lay down one's life for one's friends."[11] We tend to hurry on to Jesus's next words about being his friends by doing what he commands. But Jesus tells us that his love for us is so great that he lays down his life for us. Rather than saving us from our sins, Jesus's death and resurrection demonstrate the depth and extent of God's love for humanity and the world. Jesus lays down his life to prove and express God's self-giving, sacrificial love. We become Jesus's–and God's–friends not because of what we do for Jesus but because of what Jesus does for us. Jesus brings us "into a relationship of reciprocal love, creating a community of friends, willing to sacrifice themselves for each other."[12] This is the way of Jesus, love that results in community and justice.

Jesus's death and resurrection makes possible a change of mind and heart, brings us forgiveness, frees us from powers that would hurt us, drives out the ruler of this world who is opposed to God, demonstrates God's love, and brings new life. Jesus's death and resurrection does so much more than save us from our sins.

Other Things

Witnessing to Jesus's suffering, death, and resurrection means not witnessing to other things like ourselves, our church, and the teachings of Jesus. While we might feel these "other things" are important on their own, the way we talk about them when witnessing should highlight and illuminate Jesus's suffering, death, and resurrection.

Witnessing to Jesus is not telling our story or helping people get to know us. Witnesses are not the subject of what we share; we are the narrators and the objects of Jesus's love and saving action. We share how we experience Jesus working in our lives and also in the lives of others and in the life of the world. We can check that we are witnessing to Jesus rather than ourselves by attending to the subject of our sentences; we should say "Jesus" more often than we say "I." Too much talk of ourselves takes the focus off Jesus.

In the past, the U.S. had a predominately Christian culture, where going to church was an expected part of life in society. Therefore, it was appropriate to enlist, even emphasize, our experience of church to help other Christians understand the blessings of belonging to our church rather than another. While elements of this Christian culture remain in some places, it is not as widespread as it was and, overall, the culture and expectations of society have changed. Today, we share about the congregation, synod, and denomination to illustrate and verify what we say about Jesus. People may come to church to encounter Jesus, but only if they are intrigued by the church's radical welcome and genuine community, commitment and work for justice, and reciprocal, sacrificial love.

Finally, we must be careful how we use the teachings of Jesus. The parables that reveal God's reign are helpful, insightful, and appropriate for witnessing to Jesus because they tell who God is or what God is like. Instructions about what Jesus's disciples are to do and how we are to live are best reserved for those who already have a relationship with Jesus and wish to follow him. Telling people new to the story of Jesus what disciples are to do and how we are to live can draw their attention away from Jesus as they assess how well we are doing what we tell them Jesus expects us to do.

For Consideration and Conversation

1. Do you think we have a choice about witnessing to Jesus? Why?

2. What, if anything, prevents you from witnessing to Jesus?

3. Go someplace where you can witness something unimportant, such as people going in and coming out of the grocery store. Pay attention to what you experience and then recount it to another.

4. What do you most need Jesus to save you from? To save us from? To save the world from? Do not use church words to answer.

5. What if any way of understanding Jesus' suffering, death, and resurrection presented in this chapter appeals to you? Why?

6. Can you name an experience in your life or in your church that reveals an aspect of Jesus' suffering, death, and resurrection?

Chapter 6

Good News

The angel said to the shepherds, "Do not be afraid; for see—I am bringing you good news of great joy for all the people."[1] This first witness to Jesus announced his birth as good news for all people. Following the angel's example, we witness to Jesus by bringing good news. Ideally, the news about Jesus we bring is so good that people are filled with great joy.

Bringing good news is a choice. We can witness to Jesus in many ways. For example, John the Baptist witnessed to Jesus in a manner that warned and frightened people. John described Jesus as coming in power, axe in one hand and winnowing fork in the other, to chop down those who bear no fruit, immerse people with fire, and separate them as gathered wheat and discarded chaff. Jesus did not come as John predicted. Perhaps this is why Luke calls even John's witnessing "good news."[2]

Choosing to bring good news is important because how we witness to Jesus is as important as what we say. Asking a question demands an answer someone may not be willing or able to give, potentially shutting them down or putting them off. Instructing invites questioning we may not be able to answer. Exhortation emphasizes response and can result in resistance; John the Baptist did not tell people what to do until they asked him. Most important, witnessing in any way other than bringing good news makes the one to whom we witness, rather than Jesus, the focus of the conversation. Making the one to whom we witness our focus not only can cause that person to become uncomfortable; focusing on the person to whom we witness misses the point. Jesus is the focus of our witnessing.

As obvious as it seems, the good news we bring must be both *good* and *news*. The message is good because it has a positive impact on the one receiving it and even on the world. The announcement might be joyous, exciting, uplifting, or relieving. The message is news because it is not timeworn, tired, and familiar. The words we use might be common–Jesus brings us God's love–but the circumstances and manner in which we utter them might make them brand new.

We might ask ourselves what message about Jesus, which is both good and news, we most want and need to receive. For example, the good news that Jesus not only remembers your mother; Jesus remembers for your mother, might be the good news that someone watching their parent slip farther into dementia most needs to receive. It is good because it assures that God will not abandon us in forgottenness but will remember both us and the things we forget. It is news because this is not how we usually describe Jesus's love and salvation. "Jesus, remember me when you come into your kingdom."[3] We read, sing, and pray these words differently.

The good news must be realistic; it is grounded in everyday life. Jesus promises to bring life out of death; Jesus does not promise that anyone or anything, including the church we love, will never die but live forever. We cannot promise or guarantee Jesus will make everything turn out the way we want it to. We can promise that Jesus will be with us in everything, regardless of how things turn out. We can proclaim the good news, "We know that all things work together for good for those who love God, who are called according to his purpose."[4] This is different than telling people everything happens for a reason.

The good news is for the person with whom we share the story of Jesus. We know the difference between a generic sermon and one preached especially for a specific congregation. Ideally, the good news we bring is as particular and concrete as the one who receives it. While personally and individually knowing the one with whom we share the story of Jesus may be ideal, sometimes this is not possible. Then, we might share good news for the communities to which this individual belongs. Especially challenging is sharing good news for others that might be bad news for the one with whom we are sharing the story of Jesus. For example, Jesus's concern for the poor might not be good news for someone who is rich. In these circumstances, naming how to participate in the good news is helpful. Jesus's care for the poor becomes good news for the rich when the rich come to know the freedom and joy of using their money to join Jesus in caring for the poor.

Here we need to be careful. While we participate in God's good news, the good news does not depend upon us or upon circumstance. The good news depends upon God, made known to us in Jesus's life, suffering, death, and resurrection. If we could accomplish the good news ourselves, or if the right circumstances resulted in the good news, we would not need Jesus to save us. Since we are witnessing to Jesus, the good news is about Jesus.

We should be able to declare this good news in a sentence. It is easier when the first word of that sentence is Jesus, and the verb is a positive "action word." Our news is especially good when the ones for or with whom Jesus acts include the ones to whom we are witnessing. The good news should be detailed enough for people to understand and not be so big that it seems more like a wish, a dream, or a longing.

How We Share Good News

The angel's announcement to the shepherds helps us understand how to bring good news. The angel came to shepherds who needed good news and got their attention. Luke reports "the angel of the Lord stood before them, and the glory of the Lord shone around them."[5] We do not need anything as spectacular; we do need to get the attention of the one with whom we wish to share the story of Jesus. The simplest way might be to ask for time for a conversation.

Next, the angel extends the shepherds care by telling them not to be afraid. The angel focuses the shepherds' attention and gives them a frame of reference for what he is about to say: "for see—I am bringing you good news of great joy for all the people."[6] Providing a frame of reference helps people process what we tell them. For example, beginning a conversation by asking, "Did you hear the one about...?" signals that what follows is a joke. Starting a conversation by saying that you have some exciting, good news to share may help people not become defensive when we mention Jesus.

The angel then described the good news in detail: "Your savior is born today in Bethlehem."[7] The angel then gives the shepherds signs by which they can verify this good news: bands of cloth and a manger. Like the angel, we describe the good news in a straightforward manner and, whenever possible, point to signs by which people can verify it. Ideally, the church is one such sign. Repentance, forgiveness, and life out of death are other places to point.

Finally, the angel celebrated the good news. The angel was joined by a multitude of the heavenly host that could not contain themselves; the news was so good that they glorified and praised God and declared peace to all people. Here, the angel teaches us to respond to the good news we share. The angel shows us that sharing the good news of Jesus is like announcing your engagement or that you are having a baby, that you have been accepted to the college where you most want to go, or that you have been offered the job of your dreams.

Preparing Our Good News

"Now during those days," Luke reports, Jesus "went out to the mountain to pray; and he spent the night in prayer to God."[8] After praying, Jesus chose the twelve disciples, healed the sick and cured the troubled, and bore witness to God's reign. Though Luke does not tell us what Jesus prayed about, I suspect Jesus not only asked God who to choose as disciples, Jesus also prayed about what to say to teach the people about God's reign. Jesus prayerfully prepared his good news about the reign of God.

Even though the subject is Jesus, the good news we are preparing is not a public recounting of our conversion or religious experience. The good news we prepare is more of a written or spoken statement that gives evidence or proof of someone's character and qualifications. In this instance, that someone is Jesus. Anyone who watches legal dramas knows that even character witnesses do not take the stand without preparing. They construct and review what they will say before they testify. So, too, we prepare our good news or "testimony" before we witness to Jesus.

A straightforward and effective testimony to Jesus has four parts: (1) a firsthand or eyewitness experience of Jesus, (2) a Bible story about Jesus, (3) a declaration of good news that ties these stories together, and (4) self-discipline to relate this in an "elevator speech." We accomplish the fourth part by writing and revising the first three. Ideally, each of the three parts of this model of testimony is a well-crafted paragraph. Using this approach, high school students returning from a mission trip and lay missionaries home on leave began a two-hour seminar with a blank piece of paper and ended the seminar by orally sharing their good news testimonies with others in the group.

An Experience of Jesus: The first paragraph of our testimony is a firsthand or eyewitness experience of Jesus. We share a time in which we believe we encountered Jesus. Ideally, we choose an experience that the one to whom we witness can relate to and identify with. Then we share how we encountered Jesus in this common experience.

When witnessing to people for whom the story of Jesus is new, stories located in the home, family, neighborhood, and world are more fruitful than stories that take place in church. We can share times when we encountered Jesus as the church was at work in the home, family, neighborhood, or world. We need to be careful to share how we encountered Jesus and not how we were Jesus encountering others. Even unintentionally casting ourselves as Jesus in a story is wrought with peril and danger as people might either conclude we regard ourselves as Jesus or compare us to the claims we make about Jesus and find us wanting.

In crafting this paragraph, the goal is more than relating our experience. We want to bring those to whom we witness into the experience so that, through our words, they experience the event for themselves. To do this, we relate our story using language that produces involvement, emotions, and memories. This language is specific and concrete. It appeals to the senses. It is colored with emotions such as anxiety, disappointment, wonder, joy, curiosity, and doubt.

Description is perhaps our most useful tool. Images we relate and details we share can create the experience of the story we tell. In preparing this paragraph, we consider how to describe people, actions, and settings. We strive to use as few words as possible to keep descriptions crisp and clear; we cannot include every detail. We must decide which details will best help the one to whom we witness experience the story we share.

Some compose this paragraph sitting alone as they write a journal entry. Others tell the story aloud and either record or have a scribe write down what they say. Still others find their story by inviting someone to interview them and using a recording or transcript of the interview as the prompt for their paragraph. No approach will result in a perfect paragraph on our first try. Therefore, before we write the first word, we should plan to review and revise the paragraph several times. Think of revising as giving the Holy Spirit a chance to improve our work.

Bible Story: Next, select a Bible story about Jesus that connects with the experience we share in the first paragraph and helps us talk about who Jesus is. Gospel stories in which Jesus is the actor generally work best; however, the parables are also appropriate if we can say that Jesus is like the image or story in the parable. For example, Jesus is like the shepherd who leaves the 99 and searches for the one lost sheep. Jesus is like the woman who searches for a lost coin and, when she finds it, spends money on a party for her neighbors to celebrate. Jesus is like the father who rejoices extravagantly and throws a party when his reckless child returns home.[9]

To select a fitting Bible story, first ask yourself what stories about Jesus the first paragraph of your testimony makes you think of. Write them all down; do not choose one right away. You can also share your first paragraph with others and invite them to suggest Bible stories about Jesus. When you have compiled a list, prayerfully read, and reread the stories; ask others to read these stories and your first paragraph and tell you which they think is best and why. Eliminate stories as you go, until one Bible story about Jesus seems right to you. Then write down the reasons you chose this story.

Since you are choosing a Bible story and not a Bible text, write the story down in your own words as if you are telling it to someone. Imagining yourself telling this Bible story to a child is very effective. The goal is to master the crux, thrust, and good news of the story and not to utter every scriptural word correctly. Try telling the story to others until it seems right. When you are ready, write the story down as your second paragraph. Again, give the Holy Spirit the opportunity to improve your work through review and revision.

Good News: To create the third paragraph, read the first two paragraphs, one relating an encounter with Jesus and the other a story about Jesus from the Bible, consecutively. Ask yourself what good news about Jesus flows from these two paragraphs. The third paragraph of your testimony is the good news about Jesus that ties the two laces of the previous paragraphs together in a bow.

One way to name the good news is to allow the Bible story of Jesus to provide a perspective on your encounter with Jesus. Stories of Jesus's table fellowship can elevate family dinner from delicious to holy. The good news is that, when we pray, "Come Lord Jesus," Jesus comes to our table and home. Identifying a character from the Bible story in the story of your encounter with Jesus is another way to name the good news. For example, if the first story was about the workers at the food pantry and the Bible story is Jesus feeding the 5000, we might name the workers as Jesus's disciples distributing food Jesus provided and share the good news that Jesus continues to feed the hungry. We might then identify ways Jesus satisfies all our hungers. In addition to the good news, the third paragraph should include your response to the good news. Genuine gratitude and praise are perhaps the most compelling. Expect to review and revise as the Holy Spirit leads.

Once you have created the three paragraphs, it is important to work on transitions so the paragraphs flow from one to another. The best way to smooth your testimony is to read it aloud and, when you are ready, to read it to someone else.

Elevator Speech: People are frequently too busy, impatient, or preoccupied to devote extended periods of time to conversations and topics that do not immediately interest or benefit them. People are even more likely to dismiss or resist conversations they anticipate will challenge them or make them feel uncomfortable. Therefore, we are wise to model our testimony after an "elevator speech."

An *elevator speech* is a brief, persuasive speech that sparks interest in an organization, project, idea, product, or person. Strictly speaking, a good elevator speech should last no longer than a short elevator ride of 20 to 30 seconds, hence the name. Unless you plan to witness about Jesus to someone on an elevator, you probably have a bit more time, though not a sermon. The point is to be brief. We can say a lot about Jesus in 3 to 5 minutes, which is approximately 450-750 words.

For Consideration and Conversation

1. What was the best news you ever received? What was that like?

2. What was the best news you ever gave? What was that like?

3. What do you imagine it would be like to tell someone who really needs to hear it that Jesus loves them?

4. The time has come to write your testimony. How will you do it?

5. Who will you share the first draft of your testimony with?

6. Who will you share your testimony with when you think it is ready?

7. When will your first draft be finished?

Chapter 7

"See, I Am Sending…"

"And see, I am sending upon you what my Father promised."[1] Jesus assures the disciples that they will not witness on their own because Jesus sends the Holy Spirit upon them. Jesus's promise holds as true for us as it did for the apostles. Some contemporary disciples prepare themselves to witness to Jesus because they are confident Jesus is keeping this promise. Other contemporary disciples consider preparation to witness to Jesus to be the means by which Jesus sends the Holy Spirit upon them, as Jesus sends the Holy Spirit through preaching, baptism, and the Lord's Supper. Whatever our underlying reason and motivation, once we have written our good news testimony, we prepare ourselves to witness to Jesus. After all, witnessing to Jesus without preparing ourselves at the very least disadvantages the Holy Spirit who must overcome our lack of preparation.

We can prepare to effectively witness to Jesus in three ways. First, we can pick a partner with whom we pray, practice, and polish our testimony. Second, we can embrace our role as sowers rather than reapers. Third, we can prepare the way of Jesus, as expressed in our faith community, to welcome those who may respond to our witness. Making these preparations works best when we do not undertake them on our own. This is the time when witnessing to Jesus invites the support and participation of the faith community. As we prayerfully and faithfully practice our testimony, become comfortable with wasting seed, and ready the congregation to welcome those who may respond to our witness by coming to church, we experience Jesus sending the promised Holy Spirit to ignite us to plan and then witness to Jesus.

Pick Your Partner

"The Lord appointed seventy others and sent them on ahead of him in pairs to every town and place where he himself intended to go."[2] Jesus sent the seventy *in pairs*. What do you suppose those pairs of disciples talked with each other about as they went on their way to witness to the nearness of God's reign? They probably reacted to Jesus's "marching orders." They certainly got to know each other a bit and shared how they were feeling about this adventure, probably nervous and excited. When the conversation fell silent, I imagine one member of these pairs of Jesus's followers suggested to the other that they pray together. The prayer bolstered their courage to the point that they at first hesitantly and then more comfortably practiced what they would say to the people they were about to meet. With each practice, they refined, polished what they intended to say to make it better. Somewhere along the way, they realized what a gift Jesus had given them by sending them in pairs.

As a bishop, Craig had this exact experience walking the halls of the United States Capitol as part of an ELCA delegation and preparing for a five-minute meeting with a senator, member of Congress, or staff person to discuss a matter significant to the gospel. After dividing into pairs and making brief introductions, they prayed, practiced, and, when the time came, witnessed to Jesus in terms of the issue they came to discuss. The Holy Spirit was with them through the gift of the partner.

The time has come to pick a partner to travel alongside us on the remainder of this pilgrimage. Perhaps Jesus already assigned or revealed your partner to you. Those reading this book with someone may decide that person is your partner. Those reading this book with a group might divide into pairs or prayerfully draw names out of a hat. Luke reports Jesus appointed and sent the seventy in pairs; Luke does not report how. Nor does Luke suggest that much getting acquainted went on beforehand.

There is a special grace in partners beginning their sojourn together as coworkers who are both learning to witness to Jesus rather than as best friends. When Chelsey studied Shakespeare in college, her professor randomly assigned students a partner to have coffee with each week to discuss the assigned readings. Chelsey found not knowing her partner well at the beginning worked better because they actually did the work of talking about the text and learning together instead of idly chatting as best friends might do.

When you receive your partner, spend 10 minutes introducing yourselves to one another. Share what you are comfortable sharing about yourself at this time. You might also indicate your openness to answering questions your introduction raises for your partner. Then share how you feel about this process and intentionally witnessing to Jesus.

Pray to Invite the Holy Spirit into Your Pair

After introducing yourselves to one another, take a moment and pray together to invite the Holy Spirit into your partnership. Some people pray individually or in worship; praying one-to-one with someone is a new experience. When this is the case, the partners' first prayer together could be, "Lord, teach us to pray."[3] Jesus responded to his disciple's request by teaching the Our Father or Lord's Prayer. Partners could begin by praying this prayer for and with each other.

Jesus then tells the disciples to ask, search, and knock, and assures them our heavenly Father will give the Holy Spirit to those who ask.[4] The Holy Spirit is perhaps what those who witness to Jesus want most. So, we should ask God to give us the Holy Spirit as we prepare to witness to Jesus. We can also ask God to make us faithful, brave, and excited witnesses. We can pray that the Holy Spirit will bless and improve what we are preparing to say. We can begin now to ask God to bless and ready the ones to whom we will witness, so that they receive our testimony as good news, experience Jesus's love and life, and are filled with joy.

In those moments when we experience God sending the Holy Spirit, we pray to offer God thanks. As important as expressing our gratitude to God, these prayers of thanksgiving make us more aware of the Holy Spirit at work within and among us, especially in this time of preparation. In time, we may find that our partner is the gift and sign of the Holy Spirit for which we thank God the most.

Practice the Good News

Praying together leads partners to share their good news testimonies with each other, to practice their good news testimonies together. Initially, the goal of practicing is not to present the good news testimony perfectly or even to improve it. The goal is that we become more comfortable saying it and talking about Jesus. Before seeking feedback from each other, partners might share their own reactions to their words and how it feels to talk about Jesus.

Next, partners work together to learn and improve their testimonies by serving as each other's director and prompter. Like the director on a television or movie set, they offer prompting and feedback first on the testimony itself and in time on the way those words are presented. Depending on their level of comfort, partners might begin by reading each other's work; in time, they should listen to each other's testimony. When reacting and offering feedback, it is helpful to begin with 1 to 3 affirmations, things to be appreciated and things that were effective, and then to make 1 to 3 recommendations, things that might be reconsidered or improved.

When the partners are satisfied with their own and each other's testimonies, practicing expands, and the partners become cheerleaders and coaches for each other. Partners might offer their testimony for groups within the church or even in worship for the congregation. These testimonies would not ordinarily replace the Sunday sermon. Midweek prayer services without preaching are especially meaningful occasions for sharing these testimonies.

Partners might "test drive" their testimonies for family and friends, particularly family and friends who do not know the story or belong to the way of Jesus. The purpose is not to overtly witness to them but to enlist their assistance as members of a "focus group" or "test audience" and solicit their reactions and feedback. Of course, the Holy Spirit might be at work in these practice sessions, and our family and friends might genuinely receive the good news we share or at least become more open to Jesus. This is an added blessing and not an expectation.

In time, partners take their testimonies out of the church and practice at various places in the neighborhood. For example, partners might rehearse their testimonies for each other in a coffee shop where the other patrons can overhear their conversation. While one partner speaks, the other might be subtly attentive to people's reactions. Partners will need to be prepared to witness to Jesus should someone become curious about what they are saying and doing.

Polish the Good News

It is important to explicitly say and do what has been implied. Every round of practice should lead to polishing, to reviewing and refining our good news testimony. Some polishing involves the testimony itself. For example, we may need to change words or smooth out transitions. Other polishing has to do with the way we present our testimony. We may need to speak a little louder and try to look at the other person.

We are not able to do everything suggested to us, because the suggestions we receive often contradict each other. The best part of our testimony for some will leave others who receive it unmoved. These differing reactions and responses teach us the importance of tailoring our testimony for the one to whom we witness. We do not say things that are untrue or with which we are not comfortable. We can, however, make our testimony more thought-provoking for someone we know needs to be convinced and more heartwarming for someone else who wants to be moved. Polishing reminds us that what we have written is the basis of our testimony but the true witness to Jesus is our interaction with a specific person at a particular moment. Some aspects of witnessing are therefore beyond our control. This realization brings us back to prayer for the one to whom we witness, for ourselves, and for the presence and work of the Holy Spirit.

Sow Rather Than Reap

Jesus said to the seventy disciples he sent, "The harvest is plentiful, but the laborers are few; therefore ask the Lord of the harvest to send out laborers into his harvest."[5] Jesus's words frequently leave us confused, even disheartened, when we eagerly set out to harvest and find little if any yield. We quickly become demoralized and decide it is futile to witness to Jesus. We become nostalgic for the decades when we recall or imagine the harvest was plentiful and lament that those days are gone.

Perhaps we are so intent on reaping one crop that we completely overlook others that are ripe for the picking. For so long we assumed people who are not of another faith are Christian and so we sought to reactivate members for our churches. This is certainly not what Jesus had in mind. Jesus sent disciples to meet people where they are and assure them that the reign of God is near to them. The harvest of people wanting to be connected to God is certainly plentiful even though the harvest of members for our churches is not. We may need to survey the field differently and look for a different crop that is ready to harvest.

Perhaps the harvest is plentiful, but it is not quite time to reap. An important responsibility of harvesters is examining the plants and refraining when they are not ready to be picked. This requires patience. Jesus told a parable about a baron fig tree.[6] In this parable, the gardener who cares for the trees, watering and fertilizing them to bring them to their peak of fruitfulness, intercedes with the vineyard owner for more time to water and fertilize the fruitless tree. The gardener is patient and compassionate, which is what we are to be.

Remaining patient and compassionate can be difficult during a long growing season. Some seeds require almost continuous watering and fertilization before we notice even the smallest indication of growth. In Galatians 5:22-23, Paul includes patience among the fruit of the Spirit. As we wait for the harvest of faith in others, we are wise to ask the Holy Spirit to produce the fruit of patience in us. We pray for patience in the awareness that the gardener in Jesus's parable pointed to a time when patience would run out. The gardener said to the vineyard owner, "Sir, let it alone for one more year, until I dig around it and put manure on it. If it bears fruit next year, well and good, but if not, you can cut it down.'"[7]

Is it possible that we are laborers but not harvesters? Since Jesus sends the seventy and tells them to "ask the Lord of the harvest to send out laborers into his harvest," we might assume all the laborers Jesus sends are to be harvesters. However, Paul disagrees. In 1 Corinthians 3:6, Paul writes, "I planted, Apollos watered, but God gave the growth." The laborers Jesus sends include planters and waterers as well as harvesters. When we are disheartened and demoralized by the absence of a harvest, it is uplifting to approach our witnessing to Jesus as sowing rather than reaping. This is likely the case when we witness to people who do not know the story of Jesus. We plant the seed, someone else waters it, God brings growth, and we may not get to be the one who gathers in the harvest.

In Matthew 13:1-23, Mark 4:1-20, and Luke 8:4–15, Jesus tells a parable about a sower who went out to sow. While we tend to focus on the various soils when we consider this parable, the farmer who scatters the seed indiscriminately is the governing image for anyone who witnesses to Jesus and sows the seed of the gospel. Three-quarters of the seed the farmer scatters eventually perish. The farmer nevertheless wastefully sows the seed.

Thinking of ourselves as sowers like that farmer rather than reapers who must gather in a harvest clarifies that our labor is to witness to Jesus without taking "soil samples" and determining the likelihood the seed we plant will bear fruit for us to harvest. Jesus certainly did not calculate the yield that might result when he gave himself up on the cross. Paul observes, "But God proves his love for us in that while we still were sinners Christ died for us."[8] That we witness to Jesus without regard for any potential harvest is itself a powerful testimony to who Jesus is and what God is doing through him. As an act of faith, we witness to Jesus entrusting the growth to God and remaining patient for a harvest.

As sowers rather than reapers, we can ask ourselves how much seed we have scattered instead of how much harvest we have gathered into the church's granary. We can reflect on how many opportunities we have taken to share the story of Jesus (and how many opportunities we have missed or declined) and not how much we have produced. This is the grace of being sowers rather than reapers.

For Consideration and Conversation

1. Is there someone that you would like to accompany throughout the entire growing season, from planting to watering to harvesting?

2. How will your partner be appointed or selected?

3. What is one way your partner can help you through prayer?

4. How can your partner best give you both expressions of appreciation and suggestions for improvement?

5. What do you make of being a sower who scatters the seed of the gospel without concern for its growth or potential harvest?

6. What supports will you need so that you do not grow so impatient, disheartened, and demoralized that you give up on witnessing to Jesus?

Chapter 8

Prepare the Way of Jesus

"The voice of one crying out in the wilderness: 'Prepare the way of the Lord, make his paths straight."[1] Luke uses these words of the prophet Isaiah to describe John the Baptist; Acts describes early followers of Jesus as "belonging to the Way."[2] Isaiah's words overflow with new meaning when we consider the church or the Christian community as "the way of the Lord" or the way of Jesus. Whereas John the Baptist prepared the people to receive Jesus, the church must prepare itself to receive the people who come seeking Jesus.

The experience of the ancient church teaches us that, after or alongside an experience of God as revealed in Jesus Christ, people followed the way of Jesus by first becoming part of a Christian community, frequently as the way to meet their needs for food, shelter, and care. Over time, as providing for physical needs developed into a loving relationship, people felt a sense of belonging in a Christian community and adapted their behavior to match that of the community's. This included taking on new habits, such as prayer and almsgiving, and stopping some old habits, including worshiping pagan gods and resorting to violence. Finally, they took the community's beliefs as their own.[3]

While we seek to attract busy young families who find belonging in multiple communities, the ancient church reached out to people who needed to belong–widows, orphans, and the poor. While we make it easy for people to join (and therefore to leave) the church, the ancient church expected people to invest themselves by learning to behave differently, in ways Christians behave. While we frequently approach faith as a matter of individual mind and heart, the ancient church was convinced that believing comes from doing. Christian faith is embarking on a chosen way of life that includes belonging to the way or community of Jesus, behaving like Jesus in the world, and trusting and sharing the good news of Jesus.

People who receive the story of Jesus seek out communities that prioritize extending belonging in the name of Jesus, behaving in ways Jesus embodies, teaches, and commands, and trusting the good news of Jesus above all else. Even more disheartening and demoralizing than witnessing to Jesus and bearing no fruit is someone receiving our witness and seeking out the church to learn more about Jesus, only to turn away because what they find undermines or contradicts the good news about Jesus they received. This concerns Jesus greatly. "Jesus said to his disciples, 'Occasions for stumbling are bound to come, but woe to anyone by whom they come! It would be better for you if a millstone were hung around your neck and you were thrown into the sea than for you to cause one of these little ones to stumble.'"[4] Though Jesus here speaks of individual acts for which a particular person is responsible, occasions for stumbling can be caused by communities of faith as well. The church therefore readies itself so that those who come seeking Jesus do not stumble. Congregations not ready to authentically receive people seeking to learn more about Jesus best help them find a faith community where they can grow in belonging to, behaving like, and believing in Jesus.

Preparing the Way of Jesus

As a family gets ready to have company, preparing its home and itself to welcome visitors, so too the church must prepare itself to welcome those who may come in response to receiving the good news of Jesus. Preparing the church for company is a way those who do not consider themselves gifted to witness to Jesus can participate in this important undertaking. In fact, preparing the congregation for company is best undertaken by leaders other than those preparing themselves to witness since, ideally, the witnesses are outside the church witnessing.

The suggestions that follow offer a good start rather than an exhaustive list. Traditionally, people new to the story of Jesus seek a congregation rather than a synod or diocese, or a denomination; these suggestions are therefore focused on congregations. Yet, people might investigate a denomination's or synod's values and positions on issues, determine ones with which they resonate, and then seek out appropriate faith communities. Leaders responsible for synodical and denominational ministries are therefore wise to consider how to translate and incorporate these suggestions into their ministries.

Three questions are at the heart of the suggestions that follow. First, how well does a faith community's life together align with its confession and witness of Jesus? The ELCA vision and goal provides characteristics to consider—community, justice, and love. We have also suggested forgiveness, reconciliation, and vocation. Is Jesus the foundation and center of the community or does that place belong to someone or something else? Apart from the label "church" and a cross in a prominent place, how would people new to the story of Jesus know Jesus is the reason this community exists? Communities centered in Jesus trust God above all else, grow in God's word and rely on it as the basis of making decisions, pray, forgive, provide opportunities for people to use their gifts, and proclaim Christ in word and deed.

We can consider justice in terms of ways the community participates in the inbreaking of God's reign for all people. While it is easy for churchgoers to say they love each other, communities of Jesus manifest his reciprocal, sacrificial love for one another and for the neighbor in solidarity, advocacy, and meeting physical needs, as well as forgiveness, reconciliation, and valuing everyone's contribution.

Second, how does this community receive and accompany people desiring to follow in the way of Jesus? No prepackaged program will fit every congregation. A six-session new member class will not suffice. Since people new to the story of Jesus are not likely to show up in groups, accompanying people desiring to follow the way of Jesus will be an individual and personal experience, which is surrounded and supported by the entire congregation. We can think of the way we receive and accompany people new to the story of Jesus as a walk. This walk includes conversation about their questions and concerns that is informed by scripture. The journey is supported by prayer and facilitated by teaching how Christians walk, how Christians do and do not act as they live in the world. The journey's destination is baptism, where those new to the story of Jesus are reborn new Christians and gather around the table with Jesus' family.

The most perplexing question, perhaps, is whether we—the church or faith community—are ready to receive and accompany people new to the story of Jesus. How much we want to receive and accompany them! Yet, people new to the story of Jesus, especially people whose age and diversity make them different from us, will challenge and change us. How ready are we, individually and as a community, to change? If we are not ready, are we able to witness to Jesus and help those new to his story find a faith community that can better accompany them as they follow in the way of Jesus?

Review the Website

The congregation's website, as well as its Facebook, Twitter, and other social media presence, should exhibit the congregation's awareness that an online presence, rather than newspaper ads or the phonebook, is what people initially consult to learn about the church. Websites must be up-to-date, easy to navigate, and designed for people who do not already know or belong to the faith community. Websites can certainly provide a section for members, but making a positive "first impression" is the website's primary function.

The congregation's worship schedule, location and driving directions, and contact information should be prominent and easy to find. FAQs for visitors, including a description of what to expect, offers a gracious welcome by empowering people who may be unsure or uneasy about visiting the congregation. A section presenting the congregation's and the denomination's basic beliefs in language that is neither theological nor doctrinal presents the faith community's unique perspective on the story and way of Jesus.

Similarly, a congregation's presence on social media is an important element in connecting with those who are curious about the faith community. Social media is often used to learn more about a congregation's community, values, and mission. Therefore, posting and sharing quality content that reflects those things, is authentic to the congregation, and is relevant to the community allows those curious about the congregation to get a sense for what it is like and determine whether the congregation would be a good fit for them. Therefore, the congregation should think carefully about how their beliefs about Jesus, mission, and values are reflected in their social media posts.

Clean the House

Just as we clean the house when we are expecting company, so we clean our church building to get ready to welcome guests. We unclutter. We wash and polish. We may choose to paint and to make some minor repairs. Clean, functional, and inviting restrooms are especially important. Do not invest in sprucing up the nursery unless it will be professionally staffed. A nursery staffed by volunteers and removed from the worship space will not attract young families and inviting visitors to take their children there will make them uncomfortable. We may choose to add signage to help visitors find their way. Some resist sprucing up the church building in these ways because it makes the space a bit more public. We therefore may need to remind ourselves that the church building is God's house. Jesus asks, "Is it not written, 'My house shall be called a house of prayer for all the nations'?'"[5] God's house is always public space.

Sometimes we have trouble experiencing our church facility as visitors experience it. We therefore might benefit from asking a trusted outsider to walk through our church building and grounds with us and suggest a to-do list to help us make it more inviting. Congregations might also consider ways to make their facilities more accessible to persons who live with disabilities. In many congregations, the property committee makes this kind of tour twice a year, prior to the spring and autumn cleanup days, to determine what projects the congregation will undertake.

Open a Back Door

Some people curious about the way of Jesus may not be comfortable walking into the church building through the front door on a Sunday morning. We therefore open a "back door" to make it easier and more comfortable for them to find a way in. Back doors might include opportunities to pray or study the Bible during the week, affinity groups, and service opportunities. When prudent, gathering at a restaurant to share a meal and talk about Jesus has proven very inviting.

Whatever back doors we open, the key to those doors is connecting with those who come through them and explicitly naming Jesus in a way that indicates we know him and that he is important to us. Jesus instructs the seventy he sends, "Whatever house you enter, first say, 'Peace to this house!'"[6] Perhaps we could nuance Jesus's instruction and greet those who enter our house by saying, "The peace of Christ be with you." When we become comfortable enough with this greeting that it sounds natural, people genuinely appreciate it.

Mind Our Manners

When company is coming, parents remind children—and sometimes children remind parents—to mind their manners. As church, we also need reminding so that we do not unintentionally offend our guests. Parents tell children to say please and thank you. Churchgoers need to be told to say, "Welcome," and not to say, "You're sitting in my pew." If we are truly concerned about visitors sitting in our pews, we should return to the days of pew taxes and put family names on the pews, reserving places of honor (in the back?) for our honored guests. Jesus says, "If anyone takes away your goods, do not ask for them again."[7] When we find someone sitting in "our" pew, do not ask for it back. Instead, either ask if we might join them or experience worship from another seat.

Telling someone they are sitting in our seat implies that they have done something wrong and makes them so uncomfortable that they are likely not to return and may even get up and leave.

We should not greet someone by saying, "I don't know you!" Conversation will go better if we introduce ourselves. Moreover, while some people do not mind others reading their name tag and addressing them by name, others find instant familiarity disconcerting, particularly if they cannot read other people's name tags. With practice, people introducing themselves to others with whom they are less familiar becomes standard practice and everyone feels a bit more welcome. Similarly, we must respect guests' personal space. While some people are "huggers" most guests are protective of their personal space and are put off when hugged by an unfamiliar person, especially when they have not consented to it. Instead, offering a wave, handshake, or fist bump is an easy way to respect guests' personal space and make them feel comfortable.

We should also not leave people standing alone at coffee hour. Visitors that make the effort to find their way from worship to fellowship genuinely want to connect with someone in the congregation. Be that one. Approach people standing alone, say hello, and introduce yourself. If you discover they are visiting, you might tell them the reason you attend this church in terms of Jesus rather than, for example, the congregation's family feeling or the pastor's charm, which the visitors may have yet to experience. We might say, "I belong to this church because we are committed to meeting Jesus as we feed the hungry." Or "I worship here because I can count on hearing the good news of Jesus's love."

Using "insider language" in public speech, especially directions and announcements in worship, is impolite and excludes visitors. Jargon, shorthand language, anachronisms, and omitting details can create an unintended and unnecessary division between insiders and outsiders. Announcing that the LLG meets Tuesday at Susan's and, if you plan to attend, you should call Cheryl, assumes people understand that we are talking about the Ladies Luncheon Group, where Susan lives, and how to call Cheryl. Newcomers do not. Of course, some of the language of worship, Scripture, and faith is the mother tongue of people who belong to Jesus. Teaching those new to the story of Jesus to understand and speak this language is part of accompanying them on the way of Jesus.

Shepherds

Some congregations formally or informally provide members who shepherd visitors through Sunday morning. Some shepherds do this naturally; others are trained for this service. On their Sunday to serve, shepherds hang out before worship and watch for visitors. When visitors come to church, the shepherd welcomes them, introduces themselves, and invites the visitor to sit with them. The shepherd assists the visitor in navigating worship, including a worship folder, hymnal, and any movement during the service. After worship, the shepherd introduces the visitor to the pastor. The shepherd then invites and accompanies the visitors to the coffee hour and introduces them to other members of the congregation. To conclude their time together, the shepherd might give the visitor information about the congregation and ask for their contact information.

On the Sunday they serve, shepherds are servants of the visitor. They may not sit in their usual place or spend time with their church friends. Shepherds therefore serve in this role one or two Sundays a month. The number of shepherds serving on any Sunday depends on the number of visitors the congregation anticipates. Ideally, every visitor or visiting family receives their own shepherd so a single shepherd does not need to guide a flock of visitors. Of course, shepherds need to be attuned to visitors who are not ready for this much attention and respect their boundaries. Most shepherds find a brief training program very helpful.

Treat Jesus Like He Lives Here

Congregations ready themselves to receive company by treating Jesus as if he lives in their church building. In other words, they treat Jesus as an explicit presence rather than an implicit reference. Congregations treat Jesus as truly present in their building and faith community because visitors come to church to encounter or experience Jesus. Congregations treat Jesus like he lives here by making worship, Bible study, and prayer priorities of their life together. Visitors seek congregations that take following the way of Jesus, discipleship, and growing in faith seriously. They look for how involved members of the congregation are in these faith practices.

Congregations treat Jesus like he lives here by giving Jesus a say if not the ultimate voice in decision-making. When congregations neglect Jesus, decisions are made based on other factors, including money and cost, expediency or efficiency, and the preferences of members of the congregation. Interestingly, when members of the congregation are engaged in worship, Bible study, and prayer, and participation in these faith practices is an expected responsibility for leadership, Jesus has a very strong voice in decision-making.

Congregations treat Jesus like he lives here by explicitly naming Jesus in connection to their ministries in the community. Naming Jesus can be as simple as telling people Jesus loves them when providing meals or food. A congregation that provided winter coats to children put a note in the pocket that said, "Jesus loves you." Children were delighted to reach into their pockets and find the note. Invocation of the name of Jesus regularly results in requests for prayer. Those who serve should therefore be comfortable praying with people or someone should be appointed to pray with people who request prayer. Serving as "designated pray-er" offers people who cannot serve in other ways an opportunity to serve.

Learn About People Different from Us

Wise congregations learn about the experiences and perspectives of people who are different from themselves so they do not expect visitors, especially those who are younger and more diverse, to be like "us," and are not surprised when these visitors are not. Congregations might invite representatives of communities with which they are less familiar to lead an educational forum or event for the congregation.

While the reign of God includes all people and embraces all diversity, most congregations lack the capacity to be all-inclusive. They do well to concentrate on one or two communities in which they are interested or to which they are connected. Congregations that take small steps find Jesus have a way of using small efforts to embrace diversity to lead congregations to take larger steps and embrace greater diversity. Congregations consistently trying to welcome all people, continuing to learn and grow themselves, and, when necessary, repenting and trying again, is more important and powerful than congregations not doing anything until they can do everything perfectly.

Preparing the way of the Lord to welcome those new to the story of Jesus changes and renews the congregation. Like expectant children, we spiritually press our faces to the window watching for the company who will come. We may begin to include "our visitors" in the prayers during worship. Regardless of whether or how quickly they come, the congregation will unexpectedly realize Jesus is among them in new ways.

For Consideration and Conversation

1. How will we undertake the work of preparing the congregation to welcome people new to the story of Jesus?

2. Who will lead and oversee this important work?

3. Who is someone unknown to the congregation that we might invite to attend worship and report their experience of being a visitor here?

Chapter 9

"Stay Here in the City"

"So stay here in the city," Jesus directs, "until you have been clothed with power from on high."[1] The apostles did not wait passively. Luke reports "they were continually in the temple blessing God."[2] Acts describes the apostles "constantly devoting themselves to prayer."[3] During the "not many days from" Jesus's ascension to their getting "baptized with the Holy Spirit,"[4] the apostles also took care of scripturally mandated administrative business by electing Matthias to replace Judas as one of the Twelve.

The church's calendar marks the period between the Ascension and Pentecost as a mere ten days. Our period of final preparation to witness to Jesus is likewise short. We have come to the time when we move from preparing ourselves to intentionally witness to Jesus to planning how we will intentionally witness to Jesus, perhaps for the first time. Following the apostles' example, this time includes worship, prayer, and getting ourselves in order.

Clothed with Power from on High

In the words of Luke 24, we can think of this period of final preparation as the time when we are "clothed with power from on high." We are getting dressed or God is dressing us for the work of witnessing to Jesus. We "get ready" as an athlete does before a game, an actor does before a play, a musician does before a concert, and we all do before a night on the town. The word "clothed" suggests more than an attitude; we are wrapped in or covered with the presence and power of God, manifest in Jesus Christ and working in and through us as the gift of the Holy Spirit.

Paul urges the Ephesians to "be strong in the Lord and in the strength of his power. Put on the whole armor of God."[5] The military image of armor can be challenging, as can Paul's description of standing against the wiles of the devil and struggling against the powers of injustice and forces of evil. Still, we benefit from approaching our final preparation as the time when we fasten the belt of truth around our waist, don the breastplate of righteousness, and, for our shoes, put on whatever will ready us to proclaim the gospel of peace. We take up the shield of faith, the helmet of salvation, and the sword of the Spirit, which is the word of God, so that we stand firm with Paul as ambassadors of Christ and declare Jesus boldly.[6] During this time of spiritually "getting dressed," we can think of the Holy Spirit as our squire, valet, or lady's maid.

Set a Goal

First, we set a goal for our witnessing that we can achieve, which means we set a goal that we can control. We cannot control who or how many people will believe in Jesus or become members of the church. So, for example, the ELCA's goal is to "share the story of Jesus and the ELCA by engaging with 1 million new people."[7] Christians who belong to the ELCA can decide and control how many of that 1 million they will engage before 2025. Deciding on a number sets a goal we can track, measure, and achieve.

We can also set as our goal when we will intentionally witness to Jesus. That is, will we witness to Jesus for the first or next time within a few days, a week, a month, or longer? Waiting for the perfect moment or the Holy Spirit's irresistible prompting often means waiting forever. Waiting too long regularly results in losing our sense of urgency and our nerve; witnessing to Jesus becomes a holy intention rather than a faithful reality. Deciding that we will share the story of Jesus within a week and share the story of Jesus once weekly thereafter is a goal we can achieve. When we accomplish this goal, 52 people will have the opportunity to receive the story of Jesus in the course of a year.

Identify the Person

We sometimes have a romanticized notion that the Holy Spirit will direct someone to cross our path at the exact moment when they are most receptive to receiving the story of Jesus from us. While this is certainly possible, Jesus's own ministry suggests that we should seek people out. Jesus goes to an out-of-the-way town called Nain to seek out a widow. In Jericho, Jesus seeks out the chief tax collector Zacchaeus. Jesus tells parables about a shepherd who leaves 99 sheep to find one that is lost and a woman who searches the house for one lost coin.[8]

Who is the first person you will seek out to share the story of Jesus? People we know and care about should be among the first we consider. Think of the story of Jesus as a precious gift. Who do you most want to give it to? Think of your good news testimony as an expression of love. Who do you want to show this particular love to? While we sometimes think of someone who, in our estimation, needs or would benefit from the story of Jesus, considering the ones with whom we would most like to share the story of Jesus and people we want to honor by sharing something very important to us can be mutually graceful. The experience is like seeing something in a store before Christmas and buying it for someone because you absolutely want them to have it. How they respond to the gift really doesn't matter to you.

We often confuse sharing the story of Jesus with attempting to regain estranged members of the congregation who were once active and remain beloved friends. As much as we may miss these cherished members of our church family, inactive members of the congregation are the last people we should consider. Listening to and wooing people back to worship is a different and more difficult task than sharing the story of Jesus with people for whom it is new. Inactive church members often regard themselves as people of deep faith who know the story of Jesus, or at least the Bible, very well. They need to "talk church," to express their hurt, disappointment, disagreement, or frustration with the church. These conversations require a great deal of time and often fail to result in reconciliation or even resolution. These conversations are best undertaken by people experienced in negotiating conflict.

Including our partner as we discern the person with whom we will share the story of Jesus may be very helpful. We take care not to inappropriately reveal information about the people we are considering. Perceived gossip surely undermines our witness to Jesus. As a safeguard, we use "I" statements to name the thought behind or reason we have identified particular people as those we are considering. "I want to tell *Name* about Jesus because…"

When we have identified people to whom we want to witness, or as part of identifying those people, pray for them. Pray particularly for the person who emerges as the one to whom you will witness. Ask Jesus to come close to them, to open their hearts to a time of sharing, and to ready their lives and spirits for the good news you will bring. If you know needs and circumstances in their lives that would benefit from prayer, offer those to Jesus as well. Finally, prayerfully review your prepared testimony and polish it so that it addresses this person.

Plan the Conversation

Once we have prepared what we will say and determine who we will say it to, we can plan the conversation. We know what it is like to decide how we will share important news. We try to share good news in a manner that honors and enhances the message we bring. Think of "reveal parties" where couples disclose the sex of their baby. Regardless of how we feel about their appropriateness, reveal parties illustrate choreographing the sharing of good news.

Where will this conversation take place and how will you put yourself and the one with whom you will share the story of Jesus in that place? Will this be a special time that would benefit from an invitation: "I have something important I'd like to talk with you about. When might we find a time?" Or is it better for the topic of Jesus to come up in conversation when you and the one to whom you will witness are together naturally, over weekly coffee perhaps? As you decide, remain open to the possibility that this may be the start of a longer conversation and choose a place suitable for such a conversation.

Of course, we need to consider whether conversation is the best way to witness to this person. While conversation might be preferred, some people may become so uncomfortable that they simply shut down. Thankfully, witnessing does not need to be face-to-face. Might a letter, an audio text, or some other means of communication be the better option for sharing the story of Jesus with this individual? Meeting people where they are, facilitating their feeling comfortable and in control, and honoring how they best receive information and respond are among the factors we consider in deciding the form of our witness. If you choose not to witness face-to-face, be certain to share the reason you chose the form you did and express your eagerness to meet and have a conversation.

Self-Examination

We can be reluctant to witness to Jesus because we do not consider ourselves to be a faithful enough Christian. This concern is appropriate and valid. In our study of the gospels, we noted that Jesus's words are accompanied by actions that verify his teaching. Jesus's public ministry is characterized by healing, forgiveness, table fellowship, and service rather than domination. If Jesus needs to confirm his words with actions, we need to do so as well.

It is certainly true that people today will not know we are Christians by our love; when we do not speak of Jesus, they know only that we are loving people. At the same time, if what we say about Jesus is not accompanied and verified by expressions of Jesus's hospitality, love, and abundant life, people will be skeptical of and even dismiss what we say.

A time of genuine self-examination is in order. Neither boasting nor despairing, we simply ask ourselves how we are living our Christian faith. Where is our walk with Jesus currently taking us? How does following Jesus or being a member of the church impact the way we spend our time and money? How does Jesus reveal himself to us in our daily life, family, work, recreation, and citizenship? What place, community, or activity in which we are known could we invite the one to whom we witness to "come and see"[9] Jesus at work?

Our answers need not be overtly religious; it may be better if they are not. When our self-examination leads us beyond religion and the church, it signals our conviction that Jesus is at work in the world and our integration of our faith and relationship to Jesus into every area of our lives.

Of course, if we find areas where we feel lacking or desire to grow, we should embrace them as opportunities to "come to the unity of the faith and of the knowledge of the Son of God, to maturity, to the measure of the full stature of Christ"[10] rather than despair that we are lacking. In terms of witnessing, we can forthrightly acknowledge the gaps we find in ourselves and in the church, how Jesus directs and empowers us to address them, and what we are doing to respond.

Prayer of Blessing

When our plans are set, we are likely to experience tension in our bodies and both fear and excitement in our spirits. We are ready for our Pentecost moment. It is time to come together with our partner, pastor, and other witnesses, for prayer and blessing. Reading Luke 24:45–49 might be a filling way to begin. Someone should then pray for each witness by name. The prayer offered certainly asks God through Jesus to send the Holy Spirit upon, or stir up the Holy Spirit in each witness. We can then ask God to surround the witnesses with peace, embolden their witness, fill them with patience, and sustain them with grace. We can also pray for those with whom the witnesses will share the story of Jesus. We might conclude by praising God for the privilege of sharing the good news of Jesus. So, for example, we might pray:

Gracious and merciful God, who clothed the blessed apostles with the power of the Holy Spirit so they boldly witnessed to your love in Jesus Christ, stir up in *name* the power of your Holy Spirit, to boldly, lovingly, and faithfully witness to Jesus. Surround *name* with peace, fill *name* with patience, and sustain *name* with grace. Come close to and prepare those to whom *name* will bring the good news of Jesus. In all this, fill us with gratitude for the privilege and grace of sharing your love and abundant life in Jesus Christ, our Savior and Lord, in whose name we pray.

A prayer like this might be accompanied by the laying on of hands in blessing. Those gathered might then pray the Lord's Prayer together and safely exchange the peace. In whatever we do, we are careful not to commission witnesses to some special status, since witnessing to Jesus is the call and privilege of all who have been commissioned in baptism as children of God, heirs of God's promise, and servants of all.

Witness to Jesus

The time has come to witness to Jesus. Thank the person for meeting you and share your testimony. When you finish, you might also tell them why it is important to you that they received this good news. Take time to listen. Only if it is appropriate, invite them into further conversation or to accompany you to worship, Bible study, or prayer.

When the meeting is over, arrange a conversation with your partner to debrief. The focus here is on the witness's experience and feelings rather than the other person's response. At the conclusion of this conversation, pray together, thanking God for the opportunity to witness to Jesus.

For Consideration and Conversation

1. What is your goal?

2. With whom you share the story of Jesus first?

3. What is your plan for this conversation? Will it be a conversation?

4. What did your self-examination revealed to you that you are willing to share? How will this revelation shape and empower your witnessing?

5. How are you feeling? What else do you need to be ready?

Appendix

Session Guide

Session 1: Introduction

Read Chapter 1.

Introduce yourselves to one another.

Agree upon rules that will govern your time together, including confidentiality and respect.

Discuss Questions 1 – 4.

Session 2: The Gospels' Witness

Read Chapter 2, Sections: "He Opened Their Minds," "The Gospels," and "Similar and Unique."

Read the Gospel of Mark aloud as a group.

Discuss Questions 1 – 2.

Session 3: How to Witness

Read Chapter 2, Section: "How to Witness."

Discuss Question 3. Take turns reading the gospel story and answering the question.

Session 4: Meaningful Gospel Story

Read Chapter 2, Section: "Our Meaningful Gospel Story."
Discuss Question 4.

Session 5: Creed

Read Chapter 3.
Discuss Questions 1-3.

Section 6: Church

Read Chapter 4, Sections: "The Witness of Experience," "Tomb," and "Church."
Include a guest or video(s) to familiarize you with the witness of your synod and denomination.
Discuss Questions 1 – 3.

Session 7: Home

Read Chapter 4, Section: "Home and Family."
Discuss Questions 4 – 5.
Bring something from your home connected to an experience of Jesus. Try to avoid items that are overtly religious. Tell the group why this item is significant.

Session 8: Neighborhood and World

Chapter 4, Section: "Neighborhood," and "World."
Discuss questions 6 – 7.
Plan a "field trip" to a place in your neighborhood where you are likely to encounter Jesus.

Session 9: Witnesses

Read Chapter 5.
Ask your pastor to teach understandings of Jesus' suffering, death, and resurrection.
Discuss Questions 1-6.

Session 10: Witnesses (continued)

Use this session to complete unfinished business from Session 8.

Session 11: Good News

Read Chapter 6, Sections: "Good News," and "How We Share Good News."
Discuss Questions 1–3.

Session 12: Preparing Our Good News

Read Chapter 6, Section: "Preparing Our Good News."
Write the first draft of your good news testimony.
Discuss Questions 4-7.

Session 13: Sow Rather than Reap

Read Chapter 7.

Discuss Questions 1 – 6.

Continue working on your good news testimonies.

Session 14: Preparing the Congregation

Read Chapter 8.

Discuss Questions 1 – 3.

Share this chapter with congregational leaders to read and invite them to attend this session and participate in the discussion.

Session 15: Final Preparation

Read Chapter 9.

Discuss Questions 1 – 5.

Plan the gathering for prayer that will mark the passage from learning to witnessing.

Notes

Preface

[1] Luke 21:6.
[2] "Mission and Vision," Evangelical Lutheran Church in America, accessed September 16, 2022, https://www.elca.org/en/About/Mission-and-Vision.
[3] Evangelical Lutheran Church in America, "Mission and Vision."
[4] "About Us," The Episcopal Church, accessed September 16, 2022, https://www.episcopalchurch.org/about-us/.

Chapter 1

[1] Luke 24:52.
[2] Luke 7:17-18.
[3] Luke 2:10-12, 17-18; 24:9.
[4] Mark 16:8.
[5] Romans 10:12-15.
[6] John 12:32.
[7] John 6:65–66.
[8] "The Augsburg Confession," V, *The Book of Concord*, eds. Robert Kolb and Timothy J. Wengert (Minneapolis: Fortress Press, 2000), 40.
[9] Acts 9:2; 19:9, 23; 22:4; 24:14, 22.
[10] John 14:6.

[11] Luke 24:44-49.
[12] Luke 24:53; Acts 1:14.
[13] See Craig Alan Satterlee, *My Burden is Light: Making Room for Jesus in Preaching* (Minneapolis: Fortress Press, 2023).
[14] Matthew 6:34.

Chapter 2

[1] Luke 24:44.
[2] Luke 1:1–2.
[3] Exodus 3:14.
[4] Mark 15:34.
[5] Luke 23:46.
[6] John 19:30.
[7] Luke 10:3.
[8] Matthew 25:31-46; 28:16–20.
[9] Matthew 10:42.
[10] John 3:9–10.
[11] John 3:1-12; 19:38–42.
[12] Mark 1:32–39.
[13] Luke 14:13-14.

Chapter 3

[1] Romans 10:9; 1 Corinthians 12:3.
[2] "The Three Ecumenical Creeds," Robert Kolb and Timothy J. Wengert, eds. *The Book of Concord* (Minneapolis: Fortress Press, 2000), 19.
[3] Ambrose of Milan. Letter 42, 5. Mary Melchoir Beyenka, O.P. *Saint Ambrose: Letters.* The Fathers of the Church, Vol. 26 (New York: Fathers of the Church, Inc., 1954), 225-230.
[4] "The Augsburg Confession (1530)," Kolb and Wengert, *The Book of Concord*, 37.
[5] "The Augsburg Confession (1530)," Kolb and Wengert, *The Book of Concord*, 39.
[6] Ambrose of Milan. *Explication du Symbole*, 1. Bernard Botte. *Ambroise de Milan: Des Sacrements; Des Mystères; Explication du Symbole*, Sources Chrétienes, 25bis (Paris: Les Éditions du Cerf, 1980), 46.

7 Martin Luther, "The Small Catechism (1529)," Evangelical Lutheran Church in America. *Evangelical Lutheran Worship* (Minneapolis: Augsburg Fortress, 2006), 1162.

8 Martin Luther, "The Small Catechism (1529)," Evangelical Lutheran Church in America. *Evangelical Lutheran Worship* (Minneapolis: Augsburg Fortress, 2006), 1162.

9 Martin Luther, "The Small Catechism (1529)," Evangelical Lutheran Church in America. *Evangelical Lutheran Worship* (Minneapolis: Augsburg Fortress, 2006), 1162.

10 Martin Luther, "The Large Catechism (1529)," Kolb and Wengert, *The Book of Concord*, 434.

11 Martin Luther, "The Small Catechism (1529)," Evangelical Lutheran Church in America. *Evangelical Lutheran Worship* (Minneapolis: Augsburg Fortress, 2006), 1162.

Chapter 4

1 Luke 24:13–35.
2 Philippians 4:8.
3 Luke 8:21. Cf. Matthew 12:50, Mark 3:33.
4 Matthew f 4:17.
5 Matthew 10:7-8.
6 Luke 12:39.
7 Luke 2:12.
8 John 3:16–17.
9 John 1:10.
10 John 12:31.
11 Acts 17:28.

Chapter 5

1 Luke 24:4.
2 Matthew 11:4.
3 Luke 10:7.
4 Luke 24:46–48.
5 Luke 24:46–48. Italics added.
6 Mark 10:45.

[7] Matt Skinner. "Commentary on Mark 10:35–45." Working Preacher. October 18, 2009.

[8] John 12:30-33.

[9] Karoline Lewis. "Commentary on John 12:20–33." Working Preacher. March 29, 2015.

[10] John 13:2, 30.

[11] John 15:13.

[12] Osvaldo Vena. "Commentary on John 15:9–17." Working Preacher. May 6, 2018.

Chapter 6

[1] Luke 2:10.

[2] Luke 3:9, 16-17.

[3] Luke 23:42.

[4] Romans 8:28.

[5] Luke 2:8.

[6] Luke 2:10.

[7] Luke 2:10.

[8] Luke 6:12.

[9] Luke 15.

Chapter 7

[1] Luke 24:49.

[2] Luke 10:1.

[3] Luke 11:1.

[4] Luke 11:9–10, 13.

[5] Luke 10:2.

[6] Luke 13:6–9.

[7] Luke 13:8–9.

[8] Romans 5:8.

Chapter 8

[1] Luke 3:4.

[2] Acts 9:2; 19:9, 23; 22:4; 24:14, 22.

[3] Alan Kreider, *The Change of Conversion and the Origin of Christendom* (Harrisburg: Trinity Press International, 1999), p. xv.
[4] Luke 17:1-2.
[5] Mark 11:17.
[6] Luke 10:5.
[7] Luke 6:30.

Chapter 9

[1] Luke 24:49.
[2] Luke 24:53.
[3] Acts 1:14.
[4] Acts 1:5.
[5] Ephesians 6:10–11.
[6] Ephesians 6:10–20.
[7] Evangelical Lutheran Church in America, "Mission and Vision."
[8] Luke 7:11–17; 15:1–10;.19:1–10.
[9] John 1:39–41.
[10] Ephesians 4:13.

Bibliography

Beyenka, Mary Melchoir, O.P. *Saint Ambrose: Letters*. The Fathers of the Church, Vol. 26. New York: Fathers of the Church, Inc., 1954.

Botte, Bernard. *Ambroise de Milan: Des Sacrements; Des Mystères; Explication du Symbole*. Sources Chrétienes, 25bis. Paris: Les Éditions du Cerf, 1980.

The Episcopal Church. "About Us." Accessed September 16, 2022. https://www.episcopalchurch.org/about-us/.

Evangelical Lutheran Church in America. "Mission and Vision." Accessed September 16, 2022. https://www.elca.org/en/About/Mission-and-Vision.

Kolb, Robert, and Timothy J. Wengert, eds. *The Book of Concord*. Minneapolis: Fortress Press, 2000.

Kreider, Alan. *The Change of Conversion and the Origin of Christendom*. Harrisburg: Trinity Press International, 1999.

Lewis, Karoline. "Commentary on John 12:20–33." Working Preacher. March 29, 2015.

Luther, Martin. "The Small Catechism (1529)." Evangelical Lutheran Church in America. *Evangelical Lutheran Worship*. Minneapolis: Augsburg Fortress, 2006.

Skinner, Matt. "Commentary on Mark 10:35–45." Working Preacher. October 18, 2009.

Vena, Osvaldo. "Commentary on John 15:9–17." Working Preacher. May 6, 2018.

About the Authors

Craig Alan Satterlee is a Lutheran pastor, professor, and bishop of the North/West Lower Michigan Synod (ELCA). He was the 2019 John S. Marten Faculty Fellow in Homiletics and Visiting Professor of Theology at the University of Notre Dame, and previously professor of homiletics at the Lutheran School of Theology at Chicago. An author of ten books, he connects preaching and areas of congregational life and mission, including worship, spirituality, stewardship, community engagement, and leadership.

Chelsey Satterlee is the communications director for the North/West Lower Michigan Synod (ELCA). After graduating from the University of Michigan with degrees in English and Psychology, she managed assessments and special education in New York City charter schools. A lifelong bibliophile, she is passionate about language, storytelling, and the ways stories inspire and challenge one's understanding.